STECK-VAUGHN
Elements of Reading

Level E

Vocabulary

Isabel L. Beck, Ph.D. and
Margaret G. McKeown, Ph.D.

Read-Aloud Anthology

Steck Vaughn™

A Harcourt Achieve Imprint

www.Steck-Vaughn.com
1-800-531-5015

Acknowledgments

Literature

Grateful acknowledgment is given to the following publishers and copyright owners for permissions granted to reprint selections from their publications. All possible care has been taken to trace ownership and secure permission for each selection included. In the case of any errors or omissions, the Publisher will be pleased to make suitable acknowledgments in future editions.

p. 1, "The Dinner Party" by Mona Gardner from *The Saturday Review of Literature, 1942*. Text reprinted by permission from General Media International, Inc. "The Dinner Party" illustration by Paul Lee from *Houghton Mifflin English*, Grade 7 by Templeton, et al. Copyright © 2004 by Houghton Mifflin Company. Reprinted by permission of Houghton Mifflin Company. All rights reserved.

p. 7, *I'm a Manatee* by John Lithgow, illustrated by Ard Hoyt. Text copyright © 2003 by John Lithgow. Illustrations copyright © 2003 by Ard Hoyt. Reprinted with permission of Simon & Schuster Books for Young Readers, an imprint of Simon & Schuster Children's Publishing Division.

p. 14, From *Journal of a Teenage Genius* by Helen V. Griffith. Text copyright © 1987 by Helen V. Griffith. Used by permission of HarperCollins Publishers.

p. 25, "Elephants Can Mimic Traffic, Other Noises, Study Says" by James Owen from *National Geographic News*, March 23, 2005. http://news.nationalgeographic.com/news/2005/03/0323_050323_elephantnoise.html. Reprinted with permission.

p. 32, "Summer Days" from *Charlotte's Web* by E.B. White, illustrated by Garth Williams. Text copyright 1952 by E.B. White. Text copyright renewed 1980 by E.B. White. Illustrations copyright © renewed 1980 by the Estate of Garth Williams. Used by permission of HarperCollins Publishers.

p. 40, "An Easter Sunday Concert" excerpted from *Marian Anderson: Singer and Humanitarian*. © 2000 by Andrea Broadwater. Published by Enslow Publishers, Inc., Berkeley Heights, NJ. All rights reserved.

p. 57, "Geoffrey Pyke's Cool Idea" by Louise Gruppen, illustrated by Jan Adkins. Reprinted by permission of *Cricket Magazine*, November 2004. Copyright © 2004 by Carus Publishing Company.

p. 64, "The Wisdom of Goats" by Sandra Clough, illustrated by Wendy Edelson. Reprinted by permission of *Cricket Magazine*, May 2005. Copyright © 2005 by Carus Publishing Company.

p. 93, From *Duke Ellington* by Andrea Davis Pinkney, illustrated by Brian Pinkney. Copyright © 1998. Reprinted by permission of Hyperion Books For Children.

p. 102, "The Cat and the Golden Egg" from *The Town Cats and Other Tales* by Lloyd Alexander, illustrated by Laszlo Kubinyi. Text copyright © 1977 by Lloyd Alexander. Illustration copyright © 1977 by Laszlo Kubinyi. Used by permission of Dutton Children's Books, a Division of Penguin Young Readers Group, a Member of Penguin Group (USA) Inc., 345 Hudson Street, New York, NY 10014. All rights reserved.

p. 115, "Beetle Blisters" by Goldman Miller. Reprinted by permission of *Cricket Magazine*, September 2003. Copyright © 2003 by Goldman Miller.

p. 128, "The Tour" from *It's Not About The Bike* by Lance Armstrong. Copyright © 2000 by Lance Armstrong. Used by permission of G.P. Putnam's Sons, a division of Penguin Group (USA) Inc.

p. 143, "The Wish" from *Someone Like You* by Roald Dahl. Published by Alfred A. Knopf, Inc. Reprinted with permission of David Higham Associates Limited.

p. 152, "Blindly He Goes...Up" by Steve Rushin from *Sports Illustrated*, July 25, 2005. Copyright © 2005. Time Inc. All rights reserved. Reprinted courtesy of SPORTS ILLUSTRATED.

p. 158, "Happiness Epidemic" by David Hernandez was originally published in *Free Lunch: A Poetry Miscellany*, Issue #23 Copyright © 2000. Copyright © 2000 by David Hernandez.

p. 163, "The Mop Bucket Encore" by Diane L. Burns. Reprinted by permission of *Cricket Magazine*, January 2005. Copyright © 2005 by Diane L. Burns.

p. 173, From "GPS Technology Drives Global Treasure Hunt" retitled "Global Treasure Hunt" by Brian Handwerk from *National Geographic News*, December 1, 2004. http://news.nationalgeographic.com/news/2004/11/1130_041201_geocaching.html. Reprinted with permission.

p. 180, "La Bamba" from *Baseball in April and Other Stories* by Gary Soto. Copyright © 1990 by Gary Soto. Reprinted by permission of Harcourt, Inc.

p. 191, "The Mysterious Mr. Lincoln" from *LINCOLN: A Photobiography* by Russell Freedman. Copyright © 1987 by Russell Freedman. Reprinted by permission of Clarion Books, an imprint of Houghton Mifflin Company. All rights reserved.

p. 199, "Bicycle" from *The Color Of Water* by James McBride, copyright © 1996 by James McBride. Used by permission of Riverhead Books, an imprint of Penguin Group (USA) Inc.

Illustration

Ashley Mims pp. 14–24; Joel Spector pp. 48–56; Elizabeth Sayles pp. 83–92; Nancy Harrison pp. 115–127; Rick Powell pp. 135–142; Guy Porfirio pp. 143–151; Lyuba Bogan pp. 158–162; Robert Sauber pp. 163–172; Doris Ettlinger pp. 173–179; Stacey Schuett pp. 180–190; Marni Backer pp. 199–206.

Photography

p. 41 © Bettmann/CORBIS; p. 47 © Bettmann/CORBIS; p. 129 © Doug Pensinger/Getty Images p. 134 © Ezra Shaw/Getty Images; p. 153 © Didrik Johnck/CORBIS; p. 156 © Didrik Johnck/CORBIS; p. 192 © Bettmann/CORBIS; p. 198 Courtesy of the Library of Congress; pp. 26–27 Courtesy of Elephant Voices.org.

Additional photography by Photodisc/Getty Royalty Free and Royalty-Free/CORBIS.

Contents

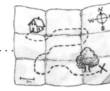

The Magic of Reading Aloud

Many literate adults have fond memories of being read to as children. This is no coincidence. Reading research has shown that, besides being an enjoyable experience, reading aloud to children is a valuable tool in the teaching of language.

How Reading Aloud Fosters Vocabulary Development

Children begin understanding a variety of words long before they can read them. A word that could provide a stumbling block to a child reading silently is perfectly comprehensible when the child hears the word spoken and used in context. It follows, then, that a Read-Aloud Anthology is the perfect springboard for vocabulary development.

What This Read-Aloud Does	What This Means for You
Exposes children to rich, sophisticated words used in captivating, age-appropriate literature selections.	You can add a large store of descriptive, robust words and concepts to children's vocabularies.
Provides engaging vocabulary introduction strategies after each read-aloud.	You can introduce the vocabulary words in natural and memorable ways as part of your read-aloud discussion.
Encourages children to relate each vocabulary word to their own experiences.	You can help children make connections with powerful words—and enjoy hearing them make the words their own!

Bringing the
Story to Life

There you are at center stage! Who, you?
A performer? Yes! Just look at your audience,
eagerly waiting for you to read them a story.
Following some simple tips will help dramatize
the performance and make it even more
satisfying and valuable for children.

Tips for Reading Aloud

Practice reading ahead of time. Reading stories and poems aloud before reading to children helps you read fluently, with appropriate intonation and expression.

Introduce the story. Before you begin reading, show children the illustrations and ask what they think the story will be about.

Build background. If you think there are concepts in the selection that will be unfamiliar, provide enough background to help children understand the reading.

Read expressively. It's difficult to overdramatize when reading to children. Don't be afraid to use plenty of expression to reflect the mood of what you are reading.

Read slowly and clearly. Listeners will be better able to absorb and comprehend what you are saying when they have enough time to form mental images as they listen.

Pace your reading. The best pace is one that fits the story events. If exciting action is taking place, speed up a bit. To build suspense, slow down and lower your voice.

Use props. Bring in or make simple props if they will help clarify or enhance the story.

Involve your listeners. Encourage children to make sound effects or to provide rhyming or repeated words when a pattern has been established.

Ask questions. As you read, ask questions that allow listeners to make connections with their own experiences and stay engaged.

Listen as you read. Pay attention to children's comments during the story so you can build on those ideas and experiences in discussions after reading.

Enjoy yourself! If you are enthusiastic about what you are reading, children will learn that reading is an enjoyable activity.

Research Says...

...regular reading aloud strengthens children's reading, writing, and speaking skills—and thus the entire civilizing process.

—The New Read-Aloud Handbook,
Jim Trelease

The Dinner Party

An uninvited dinner guest settles a debate in a most unexpected way.

Vocabulary

Words From the Story

These words appear in blue in the story. Explain these words after the story is read.

spirited	impulse
contract	arresting

Words About the Story

Explain these words after the story is read, using context from the story.

composure	perceptive
infer	refute

Getting Ready for the Read-Aloud

Show students the picture on pages 2–3. Read the title aloud. Explain that this dinner party takes place in India where snakes are common—and dangerous—visitors. Have them pay attention to the people watching the snake as it slithers toward the bowl of milk, and ask them to sum up what they see in the picture.

This story takes place in India at a time when Great Britain controlled much of the country.

Officials from the British government and officers in the military often brought their families with them to India. They tried to live life as they would back in England, but some things could not be changed.

Explain the following phrases as they occur in the story: *government attachés,* people who work for the government; *verandah,* porch; *forfeit 50 rupees,* give up money (Indian currency).

The Dinner Party

By Mona Gardner

Illustrated by Paul Lee

Highlight the conversation by using different voices. Give the colonel a very pompous voice. Act out some of the story by making a gesture to summon a servant when the hostess does and looking at each portion of the room as the American does. Speak the American's first lines very intently and stay very still for that part as everyone in the story stays very still.

The country is India. A large dinner party is being given in an up-country station by a colonial official and his wife. The guests are army officers and government attachés and their wives, and an American naturalist.

At one side of the long table a **spirited** discussion springs up between a young girl and a colonel. The girl insists women have long outgrown the jumping-on-a-chair-at-sight-of-a-mouse era, that they are not as fluttery as their grandmothers. The colonel says they are, explaining that women haven't the actual nerve control of men. The other men at the table agree with him.

"A woman's unfailing reaction in any crisis," the colonel says, "is to scream. And while a man may feel like it, yet he has that ounce more of control than a woman has. And that last ounce is what counts!"

The American scientist does not join in the argument, but sits watching the faces of the other guests. As he looks, he sees a strange expression come over the face of the hostess. She is staring straight ahead, the muscles of her face **contracting** slightly.

Why do you think the hostess' expression has changed?

With a small gesture she summons the native boy standing behind her chair. She whispers to him. The boy's eyes widen: he turns quickly and leaves the room. No one else sees this, nor the boy when he puts a bowl of milk on the verandah outside the glass doors.

The American comes to with a start. In India, milk in a bowl means only one thing. It is bait for a snake. He realizes there is a cobra in the room.

He looks up at the rafters—the likeliest place—and sees they are bare. Three corners of the room, which he can see by shifting only slightly, are empty. In the fourth corner a group of servants stand, waiting until the next course can be served. The American realizes there is only one place left— under the table.

His first **impulse** is to jump back and warn the others. But he knows the commotion will frighten the cobra and it will strike. He speaks quickly, the quality of his voice so **arresting** that it sobers everyone.

"I want to know just what control everyone at this table has. I will count three hundred—that's five minutes—and not one of you is to move a single muscle. The persons who move will forfeit 50 rupees. Now! Ready!"

The 20 people sit like stone images while he counts. He is saying ". . . two hundred and eighty . . ." when, out of the corner of his eye, he sees the cobra emerge and make for the bowl of milk. Four or five screams ring out as he jumps to slam shut the verandah doors.

"You certainly were right, Colonel!" the host says. "A man has just shown us an example of real control."

"Just a minute," the American says, turning to his hostess, "there's one thing I'd like to know. Mrs. Wynnes, how did you know that cobra was in the room?"

A faint smile lights up the woman's face as she replies: "Because it was lying across my foot."

What do you think the American will do now that he knows there's a snake under the table?

Talking About the Story

Ask students how they think the colonel felt when he found out a woman was the first to know the snake was there but she showed complete control.

Ask students what they would do if a poisonous snake was on their foot.

Vocabulary in Action

Words From the Story

spirited

In the story, the conversation between the young woman and the colonel was spirited because they were both defending their opinions. A spirited action is one that shows great energy and courage.

- Ask which is a spirited story, an energetic adventure or a slow-moving drama. Why?
- Have students say some things that they are spirited about.

contract

The muscles of the hostess' face contracted when she felt a snake under the table. If something contracts, it pulls together or becomes smaller and shorter.

- Ask students who is contracting themselves, the boy who hugs his knees to his chest or the boy who's spread out on the floor. Explain your answer.
- Have students spread their arms wide and then contract them.

impulse

The American had an impulse to jump back from the table. An impulse is a sudden desire to do something.

- Ask which is an impulsive decision, something that has been planned for two weeks or something decided upon in two minutes. Explain.
- Have students tell what their first impulse would be if a frog was dropped down the back of their shirt.

arresting

The intense tone in the American's voice arrested everyone's attention. Something that is arresting grabs your attention so much that you stop what you're doing.

- Ask students what type of behavior they might consider arresting, a person who suddenly does ten jumping jacks in the middle of a test or a person who quietly reads a book in the library. Why is that?
- Have students take turns trying to speak in an arresting manner.

Vocabulary in Action

Words About the Story

composure

The hostess sat very still even though the snake lay across her foot. You could say that she kept her composure. Someone with a lot of composure appears calm and controls their feelings, even in difficult situations.

- Ask who is showing composure, the girl who gets the fire extinguisher when there's a fire or the girl who just screams. Why?
- Ask students to name some times when they have lost their composure and some times when they have kept it.

infer

The American guessed that a snake was under the table by watching what was taking place in the room. You could also say that he inferred that the snake was under the table. If you infer that something is the case, you figure out that it is true based on what you already know.

- Ask students when they might infer that there's a runaway dog, when seeing a person walking a dog on a leash, or when seeing a person carrying a leash and calling "Here, Spot. Come here." Explain.
- Ask students what they inferred about the story after looking at the picture on pages 2–3.

perceptive

The American watched the other guests carefully. People who are very aware of the people around them are sometimes called perceptive. A perceptive person is good at noticing or realizing things that are not obvious.

- Ask students when they might need to be perceptive, while crossing a busy street or while laying on the beach. Why is that?
- Ask students what things around the classroom a perceptive person might notice.

refute

The colonel's argument was proven wrong when the hostess did not scream or yell even though a snake was lying across her foot. You might also say that his opinion was refuted. If you refute something, you prove that it is wrong or not true.

- Ask who is refuting something, the person who explains that the world is not flat but is actually round or the person who explains the plot of their favorite movie. Why do you think so?
- Have students refute the statement that the sky is green with pink polka-dots.

I'm a Manatee

In this fanciful poem, a young boy describes the engaging manatee and its underwater world with silly but vivid detail.

Vocabulary

Words From the Poem

These words appear in blue in the poem. Explain these words after the poem is read.

undulate	stately
modest	encumbered
immune	

Words About the Poem

Explain these words after the poem is read, using context from the poem.

placid	endearing
whimsical	

 Getting Ready for the Read-Aloud

Show students the picture of the boy and the manatee on pages 8–9. Read the title aloud. Have students notice that the boy sees a manatee when he looks in the mirror. Also point out that the boy has drawn several pictures of manatees that hang on the wall near the mirror.

Explain that manatees have existed on the planet for millions of years. They are very large—adult manatees reach 8 to 13 feet in length and weigh up to 3,650 pounds. Some people think they are ugly, and they certainly are very wrinkly, but they are extremely gentle. They eat plants and other vegetation. Sometimes they'll approach swimmers or small boats looking for rubs and scratches. They are an endangered species with humans as their only known predators.

The following phrases occur in the poem and can be briefly explained as you come to them: *unshackled by the chains of idle vanity*, not worried about personal appearance; *human folly and inanity*, stupidity; *herbivore*, a vegetarian or plant-eater; *dietary habits*, what you eat; *cuisine*, food; *wit, sophistication, and urbanity*, clever, elegant, and polite; *profanity*, bad words; *humanity*, people.

I'm a Manatee

By John Lithgow
Illustrated by Ard Hoyt

Read this poem using lively expression and vocal variation, emphasizing the poem's cadence. Read it with the excitement, silliness, and enjoyment of a child in a made-up adventure.

From time to time I dream
That I'm a manatee,
Undulating underneath the sea.

Unshackled by the chains of idle vanity,
A **modest** manatee, that's me.

I look just like a chubby brown banana-tee
As I nose along the cozy ocean floor.
Immune from human folly and inanity,

That's why a manatee
Is such a happy herbivore.

I'm a manatee, I'm a manatee.
I'm every bit as wrinkled as my grann-atee.

No difference between my face and fann-atee,
A noble manatee, that's me.

With the dietary habits of a manatee,
I never fail to lick my platter clean.

I sprinkle seaweed on my Raisin Bran-atee,
The perfect manatee cuisine.

> That might be perfect manatee cuisine, but I sure wouldn't want to eat it!

With my wit, sophistication, and urbanity,
I dignify my watery domain.

No one near will ever hear me use profanity,
Because a manatee has his image to maintain.

I'm a manatee, I'm a manatee.
I keep my reputation spick and span-atee.

No difference between my face and fann-atee,
A **stately** manatee, that's me.

Encumbered by my lumbering gigan-atee,
I'm thought to be an ocean-going brute!

The least appealing creature on the planet-ee,
But to a manatee, I'm cute!

I prefer my world of silence and of sanity,
But my underwater friends don't all agree.

For whenever I am dreaming I'm a manatee,
Somewhere a manatee is dreaming that he's me!

Do you think animals ever dream of being human?

I'm a manatee, I'm a manatee,

Outside the fold of boring old humanity.
No difference between my face and fann-atee . . .

I'm a roly-poly,
Jelly-rolly,
Sugar-bowly,
Heart-and-soully
Manatee . . .

That's me!

Talking About the Poem

Ask students why the narrator imagines he is a manatee.

Ask students if they have ever imagined being a specific animal. What did they imagine they were?

Vocabulary in Action

undulate

A manatee undulates when it swims. If something undulates, it moves or is shaped in gentle waves, like the movement of water.

- Ask students when they might see someone undulate, when they are watching hula dancers or when they are watching a car race. Explain.
- Have students undulate by imitating the motion of seaweed under the water.

modest

The manatee is modest because it is not concerned about how it looks. Someone who is modest doesn't brag about things they can do or things they have done.

- Ask which person might be more modest, a girl who tells everyone about her latest accomplishment or a girl who keeps her accomplishments to herself. Why is that?
- Have students decide if they are modest or not.

immune

In this poem, manatees are immune to the stupid things that humans do. If you are immune to something, you are not affected by it.

- Ask students what they would rather be immune to, winning the lottery or getting the chicken pox. Why?
- Have students name some things that they would like to be immune to and some that they would not like to be immune to.

stately

Manatees are stately creatures. Someone or something that is stately is impressive and grand in size or the way they act.

- Ask which type of building might be considered stately, a large old mansion or a small grocery store. Explain your answer.
- Have students walk in a stately manner across the room.

encumbered

Because they are encumbered by their gigantic size, manatees move slowly. If you are encumbered by something, it limits your movement or keeps you from doing what you want.

- Ask students when they are encumbered, when hauling a backpack filled with textbooks or when carrying an empty backpack. Why do you think so?
- Have students name some other things that might encumber a person.

Words About the Poem

placid

Manatees are very calm creatures. Another way to describe them is placid. A placid person or animal is calm and doesn't get easily excited, angry, or upset.

- Ask students which day would be more placid, a relaxing day on the beach or a busy day rushing from place to place. Why?
- Have students decide if they are placid or not.

whimsical

This poem is silly and fun. You could also say that the poem is whimsical. Someone or something that is whimsical is playful and surprising.

- Ask what type of story might be whimsical, a news report about business or a song about dancing with bears. Explain.
- Have students name some other whimsical stories or poems they have heard.

endearing

People who understand the characteristics of manatees really like them a lot. You might also say that people find them endearing. If you call something a person does endearing, you mean it makes you feel fond of them.

- Ask students which child is more endearing, the little brother who breaks his sister's favorite CD or the little brother who draws a special picture for his sister. Why is that?
- Ask students if they have pets with endearing habits. What are they?

Journal of a Teenage Genius

In this humorous story, a teenage genius wishes his parents were more enthusiastic about his interest in science, until one day, when an experiment has surprising results.

Vocabulary

Words From the Story

These words appear in blue in the story. Explain these words after the story is read.

sufficient	defer
mishap	wrath

Words About the Story

Explain these words after the story is read, using context from the story.

hilarious	dabble
likeness	ordeal

Getting Ready for the Read-Aloud

Show students the picture of the teenage genius on page 15 and read the title aloud. Explain that scientists use this type of equipment in their labs. Have them notice the look in the boy's eyes and what he is wearing.

Explain that this is a fiction story about a teenage boy who wants to be a scientist. Tell them that real scientists mix chemicals together, but they usually know how they will react with each other. They also put safety first, and when they aren't sure how chemicals will react, they are extra cautious.

Some words and phrases in the story may be new to students. You can briefly explain these as you come to them: *beaker over my Bunsen burner,* glass container over a small, tube-shaped stove; *matter,* anything that has mass and takes up space; *lack of foresight,* inability to look ahead; *salvage,* save from the wreckage; *bewildered,* confused.

Journal of a Teenage Genius

from *Journal of a Teenage Genius*

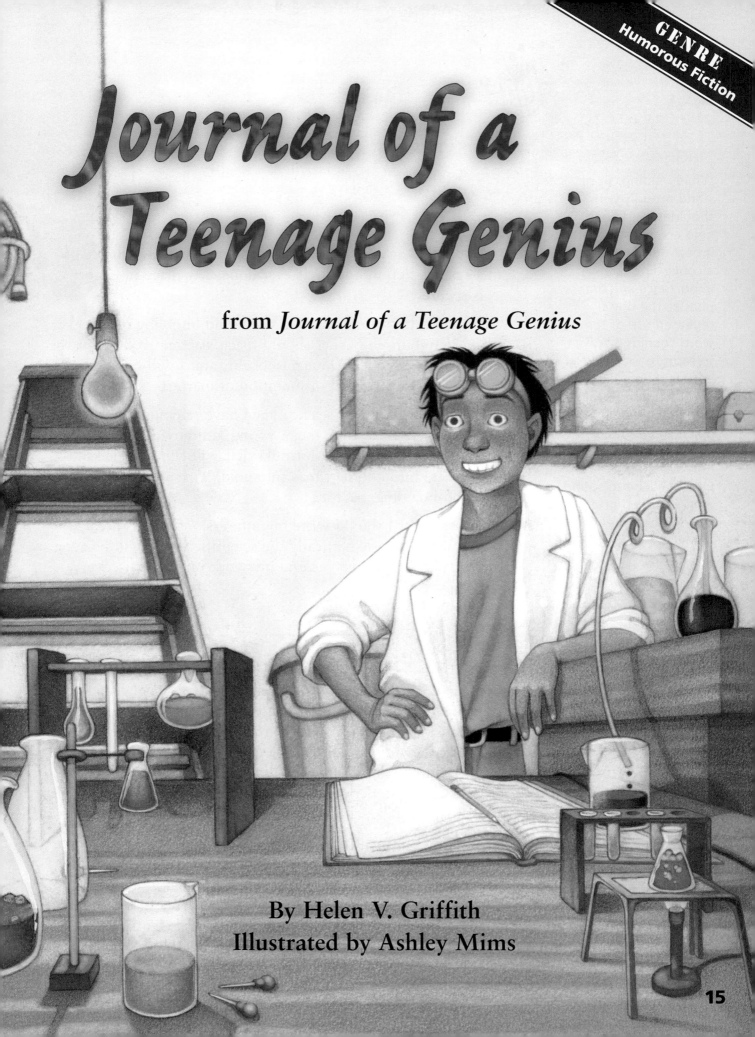

By Helen V. Griffith

Illustrated by Ashley Mims

15

Bringing the Story to Life

While reading, sit or stand proudly with shoulders and head held erect. Use vocal inflection to convey a comic air of self-importance and emphasize the boy's repeated use of the word "genius." Try to capture the indignation in lines like "my own mother has turned me out of our own basement," and "she'll realize how wrong she was." Later, be sure to sound a bit panicked after the dog becomes a boy!

What is the narrator's opinion of himself?

SATURDAY, AUGUST 20
9:00 A.M.

Success at last! I have achieved what nobody outside of a science-fiction novel has ever done! My place in history is secure.

In another fifteen minutes the liquid bubbling in a beaker over my Bunsen burner should reach **sufficient** heat for the necessary chemical change to occur, and I will have invented the formula for the transmutation of matter!

Since the dawn of science, men have attempted to discover this secret, but it took me, a young, unknown genius, to finally come up with a formula that will change one kind of metal into another. Iron into gold! Tin into silver! Wow! Mind-boggling, isn't it?

I feel that I should write my impressions of this great moment, because naturally the scientific world will be agog with curiosity about me and my work once my discovery comes to light.

First, some background. It's been a long, lonely road, and being a genius really isn't as great as you might think, mainly because nobody else takes you seriously. My mother, for instance. My mother, *especially*. She keeps saying that I don't understand what I'm doing, that it's dangerous, that I should perform my experiments in school with supervision. In other words, she talks as if I'm just an ordinary kid playing with a chemistry set.

I am working under very difficult conditions in our un-equipped, poorly lit garage because my own mother has turned me out of our own basement, just because of a few minor **mishaps** that could happen to any scientist.

Such as the odor from one of my earlier experiments forcing us all to leave the house for the weekend.

> Does that sound like a minor problem to you?

But did I complain? Even though it set me back in my work, I put up with the inconvenience and relaxed and enjoyed swimming in the motel pool.

My parents weren't such good sports, though. My mother even claimed the smell made Toodles sick. As if anything could get Toodles down. My mother worries over him as if he were a baby, and he's just a hyperactive little poodle. I think we probably would have stayed home that weekend, smell and all, if it hadn't been for Toodles.

The latest incident is the one that drove me from my basement lab, and the whole thing was Toodles's fault. He was watching me work, like the nosy little mutt he is, and just as I picked up a test tube of one of my chemical solutions, he jumped up on my leg to get a better look and I spilled the stuff right in his face.

You never heard such yelping in your life. And you never saw the mother of a teenage boy move so fast. She was down those basement stairs in about two leaps, sized up the situation in an instant, and, brushing aside my reassurances that the chemical—although irritating—was not dangerous, she stuck Toodles in the sink and turned the water on him.

After she washed him off he quit yelping and just stood there shivering and looking about half his size. I would have welcomed a quiet discussion of my mother's misunderstanding of the danger involved, but she kept saying things like, "That does it" and "This can't go on" and "That kid," so it seemed wise to **defer** any more explanations and to move my equipment before she did something that we would both regret.

When my journal is made public, she'll realize how wrong she was, and though I'm sorry the world has to know of her lack of foresight, still this is a factual account of the greatest scientific breakthrough of the age, and it may be an encouragement to other geniuses not to give up just because their mothers don't have faith in them or appreciate their abilities.

At this moment the solution in the beaker is bubbling away like crazy. I must record this while it is happening. It's turning wild colors and boiling and steaming and—oh, wow—it almost looks like it's going to . . .

SAME DAY, 10:00 A.M.

It did. And I'm in big trouble.

> What do you think happened to the solution?

I'm writing this in my room where I have come to escape a mother's **wrath**. She keeps saying, "You could have been injured, maybe even killed," and she's not even concerned that the greatest scientific discovery of the age just blew up.

There wasn't really that much damage, anyway. I mean, what's a broken window? The real disaster is that I failed. And my notebook with all my calculations in it is gone, destroyed in the explosion.

The work of years is now a puddle on the garage floor, and it doesn't take a genius to know that my experimenting days are over, at least around here. My father will be less than joyful when he sees the garage, and my mother is overreacting, as usual.

She must be calming down somewhat, though, because I can hear her calling her precious Toodles. If anything can cheer her up, he will.

> Does the narrator's mother care a lot about Toodles?

And so, fellow scientists, I shall take this opportunity to return to the garage and see what I can salvage.

SAME DAY, 11:00 A.M.

Scientists of the world, what I have to report now is going to set you all on your ears.

As I slipped into the garage I almost stumbled over a little curly-haired boy about five or six years old who was sitting all huddled up on the floor, wearing a bewildered expression and nothing else.

"Who are you?" I asked. "Are you lost or something?"

The little boy's lips started to quiver and he said, "I'm Toodles."

Being a genius, a horrible suspicion of the truth dawned on me instantly, but I said skeptically, "What do you mean, you're Toodles?" and right away the little boy started to cry out loud, and between sobs he said, "I *am* Toodles, only there's something wrong with me. I came in to look around and I found a nice puddle on the floor and I lapped it up and then I felt funny and all at once my fur was gone and I'm cold. And my nose is dry."

> What happened to Toodles?

Well, you can imagine my amazement, not to mention my consternation, because my experiments in the transmutation of matter were not for the purpose of turning little dogs into little boys, but evidently that is just what has happened.

Some words of my mother's about danger and fooling with things I don't understand sneaked into my brain, but I pushed them out again. How could it be wrong to try to advance scientific knowledge?

Looking at Toodles, though, crying tears all over the garage floor, I saw that there was more to science than cold facts. I hadn't given any thought to what effects my experiment might have. I'd had no idea it would work on living creatures. And if there was a way to reverse the process, I hadn't discovered it yet.

And now my normally nimble brain seems to be clogged with molasses. I can't really grasp what has happened, much less predict the consequences.

All I've done so far is sneak Toodles into my room and dress him in some old stuff of mine. Everything is too big, but that can't be helped. Nobody noticed he wasn't wearing clothes when he was a furry little dog, but now it's obvious to the most casual observer.

At this moment Mom is combing the neighborhood for the dog-Toodles, while the boy-Toodles is here being his usual busybody self, only on two legs instead of four. He's having a great time going through my bureau drawers, something he wasn't able to do when he had only paws, and he seems contented enough at the moment, at least. But what am I going to do with him? How will I explain him? Without the formula to prove my story no one will believe the truth, I know that. They'll probably think I'm a kidnapper. I can see it now—like those old movies on TV—me, in a hard chair in the middle of a bare room, bright lights blinding me, harsh voices saying over and over, "Okay, talk. Where did you get the kid?" and me saying, "He's my mother's poodle."

Is the teenage genius staying calm?

As you can see, the situation is impossible. Not to mention that I seem to be losing my grip. I must not panic. There has to be a sane, reasonable way out of this mess.

Poor Mom. I can hear her in the yard now, calling Toodles. I know she's worr—

SAME DAY, 12:00 NOON

That was close. When Toodles heard my mother's voice, he took off down the hall like a shot, but I grabbed him and dragged him back here and we came to an understanding. I hope.

I told him that for the time being his name is Tommy, he's new in the neighborhood, and he's a *boy*. I guess he understands what I mean. He just said, "Okay," and then curled up in a ball on the floor and sighed.

My mother is calling me for lunch. This is the moment of truth. Will Toodles act the way I told him, or will he drink out of his bowl on the floor? Will Mom recognize Toodles in human form? Will she notice that the clothes he's wearing are mine? And will I break out into the hysterical laughter I feel coming on?

If this is the last notation in my journal, you can draw your own conclusions.

SAME DAY, 1:00 P.M.

Fellow scientists, Toodles cannot be depended on. He is not a boy, he is a two-footed poodle.

As soon as we entered the kitchen, he ran to my mother, wrapped his arms around her knees, and looked up at her adoringly with his big brown eyes.

> Why does Tommy do this?

"Why, who is this?" said my mother. "What a cute little boy."

I told her my prearranged story and felt like a rat for lying, although it wasn't totally a lie, he was a new kid in town. Then Mom told me about Toodles being gone and how worried she was and I felt like a *double* rat.

We got through lunch somehow, but it was touch and go, especially as Tommy showed a tendency to lap his soup and afterward asked for a biscuit. Fortunately my mother thought he meant a cookie.

After he ate his cookie he sat on the floor by my mother's chair and put his chin on her knee. With those brown eyes and that mop of curly hair he looked so much like the original Toodles that I didn't see how my mother could help but notice.

She didn't, though. She just looked kind of surprised and said, "Such a friendly child. Do you go to school, Tommy?"

Toodles said, "No, but I'm smart. I can sit up, roll over, and shake hands."

Before he could demonstrate, I grabbed him by the wrist and pulled him out of the room after me, muttering something about reading him a story.

And now here I am back in my room trying to calm Toodles, who is whimpering that he is cold and that everything feels wrong.

Poor Toodles. I've really messed up his life, not to mention how bad my mother feels without her little dog. I'm beginning to think I never should have tried such a risky experiment by myself. I should have anticipated the possibility of something going wrong and been prepared for it. I should have listened to my mo—no, I won't go that far.

Enough of these recriminations. Away with this self-pity. Am I a genius or a clod? I have things to do. I have to set up a new lab somewhere. And I need a place to hide Toodles while I work on an antidote. In the meantime he stays locked in my room. I'm afraid of what he might do if he saw a cat.

Talking About the Story

Have students name some things that happened as a result of the teenage genius's experiments. How did these things affect his family?

Ask students to tell about a mistake they made that didn't seem funny when they made it, but that they laugh at now.

Words From the Story

sufficient

In the story, the liquids need sufficient heat in order for the experiment to work. If you have a sufficient amount of something, you have as much of it as you need.

- Ask students what a sufficient amount of candy would be, a full bag or an empty bag. Why?
- Have students give sufficient proof that they have tongues.

mishap

The main character's mishaps in the basement got him kicked out of there by his mother. If you have a mishap, something has happened to you that is bad, but not serious.

- Ask students which situation they would consider a mishap, a serious car accident or a spilled glass of milk. Explain your answer.
- Have students describe mishaps that have happened in their lives.

defer

When a chemical spilled on Toodles, the teenage genius decided to defer explaining what happened since his mother was still very angry. If you defer something, you put it off until another time or pass it off to someone else.

- Ask students which activity they would choose to defer, raking and bagging all the leaves in the yard or listening to their favorite song. Explain why.
- Have students name a place they would like to defer going to and tell why.

wrath

When the liquid in the beaker explodes, the main character goes to his room so he does not have to face his mother's wrath. If you are experiencing someone's wrath, they are very mad at you.

- Ask students when you might be wrathful, when someone asks you for help with homework or when someone helps themselves to your homework. Explain.
- Have students practice showing their wrath with facial expressions and body language.

Vocabulary in Action

hilarious

Some people may have laughed at the things that the main character did to Toodles and his parents. In other words, they may have thought it was hilarious. Something hilarious is very funny.

- Ask what type of movie is more likely to be hilarious, one about three funny strangers stranded on a volcanic island or one about what happens when a volcano erupts. Why?
- Have students practice reacting to something hilarious using facial expressions and body language.

likeness

The boy-Toodles looks very similar to the dog-Toodles. Another way to say that is that they share a likeness. If two things or people have a likeness to one another, they look a lot alike.

- Ask which pair of people is most likely to share a likeness, a father and son or two complete strangers. Why do you think so?
- Have students talk about who they share a likeness with.

dabble

The teenage genius might disagree, but his mother would probably say that he does not know everything about science. In other words, she would say he dabbles in science. If you dabble in something, you enjoy doing it from time to time, but you aren't an expert.

- Ask students who dabbles in art, someone who doodles in the margins of their notebook or someone who sells their paintings at art shows. Explain your answer.
- Have students name some things they dabble in.

ordeal

Becoming a boy and learning to act like a human being must be difficult for Toodles. Another way to say that is that it is an ordeal for Toodles. An ordeal is something bad that happens that is hard to go through.

- Ask students when they might go through an ordeal, when they go to the ice cream shop or when they go to the hospital. Explain.
- Have students think of other situations that could be considered ordeals and tell why.

Elephants Can Mimic Traffic

People can make a lot of sounds and some birds can imitate human speech, but who knew that elephants can mimic traffic noises?

Vocabulary

Words From the Story

These words appear in blue in the story. Explain these words after the story is read.

capable	**distinguish**
emanate	**tendency**

Words About the Story

Explain these words after the story is read, using context from the story.

detect	**revelation**
mundane	**elicit**

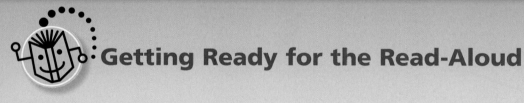

Getting Ready for the Read-Aloud

Show students the picture of zoologist Joyce Poole with the elephants on pages 26–27. Read the title aloud. Explain that Poole is a scientist who studies elephants in Africa. Explain that this is an informative nonfiction article that tells about her most recent discovery.

Tell students that nonfiction articles are written to inform people about interesting facts. Explain that elephants are fascinating animals that people don't understand. Because they don't understand them, people like Poole study elephants to learn more. This article tells about a new and surprising discovery about elephant behavior.

The following words and phrases occur in the story and can be briefly explained as you come to them: *vocal imitation,* copying sounds with your voice; *zoologist,* a person who studies animals; *mimicry,* imitation; *unelephantine,* not elephant-like; *the savanna,* open grasslands; *repertoire,* set of abilities; *replicating,* copying.

Elephants Can Mimic Traffic

By James Owen

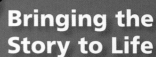

It isn't only children playing with toy cars who make engine noises. Elephants produce a similar roar, though in their case it's the rumble of trucks on an African highway that the animals imitate, scientists say.

The experts behind the discovery say elephants are **capable** of vocal imitation, joining a select group of animals that includes parrots, songbirds, dolphins, and humans.

Read the article with a light tone of voice to maintain student interest and let the facts emphasize themselves. Use a humorous tone of voice as appropriate for phrases such as: "rather unelephantine noises," and "Mlaika might simply like the rumble of trucks."

Zoologist Joyce Poole was the first to notice some rather unelephantine noises **emanating** from a group of semiwild, orphaned elephants in Tsavo National Park, Kenya. She managed to track the sounds to a female named Mlaika. But the ten-year-old's powers of mimicry were so developed that the task wasn't easy.

"I was sometimes unable to **distinguish** between the distant trucks and Mlaika's calling," said Poole, the scientific director of the Amboseli Elephant Research Project. "This is what first made me wonder whether she could possibly be imitating the truck sounds."

What made it difficult for Poole to find Mlaika?

Poole said others in Mlaika's group have been heard to make a similar noise, which is quite different from any call previously recorded in elephants.

Poole suspects Mlaika began mimicking traffic on the busy Nairobi-Mombassa highway because she got bored in her nighttime stockade located two miles (three kilometers) away from the road. "It was a sound she heard every night. Just after sunset sound travels well on the savanna."

Another possible explanation is that Mlaika might simply like the rumble of trucks. "Perhaps it was pleasing to her in some way, like humming is to us," Poole speculated.

Like humming a song except it's car noises!

Whatever the motivation, the main point, Poole said, is that elephants can actually produce such a sound.

"It shows they are able to come up with novel sounds outside their normal repertoire—some of which they have learned through imitating other animals or machines," Poole said. "This is extremely unusual for mammals."

Studies suggest some other group-living mammals may mimic unusual sounds for similar reasons. For instance, sperm whales have been found to match the click repetition rates of submarines' sonar signals. And captive bottlenose dolphins have shown themselves to be skilled at replicating computer-generated sounds.

The best known mimics in the animal world are birds. Pet parrots and mynah birds, in particular, are famous for their ability to copy words and expressions taught to them by their owners.

Birds also have a **tendency** to pick up on mechanical sounds. Elephants might be good at truck noises, but Australia's lyre bird can imitate motorcycles, chain saws, and clicking cameras. Other Australian birds are including cell phone ring tones in their repertoire.

The ring-tone phenomenon has also been noted among songbirds in Britain, another country with high numbers of cell phones per capita.

According to the Royal Society for the Protection of Birds, Europe's largest wildlife conservation charity, mimicry accounts for around 10 percent of the songs of the European starling. Ring tones, car alarms, and other electronic noises feature in its hit parade.

Similarly, song thrushes, blackbirds, and marsh warblers in the U.K. are incorporating such sounds into their songs.

Studies indicate that, for birds, vocal copying may improve a male's ability to attract mates and defend its territory from rivals.

Yet the elephant's reputation as a mimic is set to grow. "I know someone who owns an elephant that makes a humming sound that he thinks it learned from listening to a lawn mower," Poole said. The researcher also knows of "croaking" elephants that might possibly be imitating frogs.

She added, "We are due for some more surprises from elephants—a species that continues to surprise!"

Talking About the Story

Have students tell what the article was about and what they learned from it.

Ask students if they've ever seen an elephant in person. Ask students if they can remember what sounds the elephant made.

Vocabulary in Action

capable

The story tells us how elephants are capable of imitating sounds. You are capable of doing something if you are able to do it.

- Ask students who is more capable of doing a job, someone who has been trained for it or someone trying it for the first time. Why is that?
- Have students name some things they are capable of and some things they are not capable of.

emanate

The sound of a truck emanated from one of the elephants in the story. If a sound or feeling emanates from somewhere, it comes from there.

- Ask where music might emanate from, a radio or a sleeping dog. Explain your answer.
- Have students describe some smells that emanate from different foods.

distinguish

Joyce Poole sometimes found it difficult to distinguish between the trucks and the elephant imitating them. If you can distinguish one thing from another, you can tell the difference between them.

- Ask what distinguishes a chocolate chip cookie from a sugar cookie, chocolate chips or flour. Why do you think so?
- Have students name some things that make it easy to distinguish them from their peers.

tendency

The birds mentioned in the story have a tendency to imitate mechanical sounds. If someone has a tendency to do something, it means they are likely to do it.

- Ask which girl has a tendency to bite her nails, the one who bites her nails when she's nervous or the one who never bites her nails. Why?
- Have students tell what activities they have a tendency to participate in.

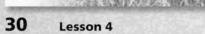

Words About the Story

detect

Poole noticed one of the elephants making a strange sound. You might say that Poole detected the sound. If you detect something, you notice it or sense it, even if it is not very obvious.

- Ask students which person appears to have detected something, the one who continues to walk toward the snarling jaguar or the one who says "ooh, I think I'll go a different way." Explain your answer.
- Have students try to detect something at their desk they've never noticed before.

mundane

Some animals copy everyday sounds. Another way to say that is that they copy mundane sounds. Something that is mundane is very ordinary, not at all unusual or interesting.

- Ask which activity is mundane, hanging out at home or going to the moon. Why do you think so?
- Have students describe a mundane day.

revelation

Before Joyce Poole, no one knew that elephants could mimic some of the sounds they heard. Another way to say that is that it was a revelation. A revelation is a surprising or interesting fact that is made known to people.

- Ask what would be considered a revelation, the discovery that the earth is made of rock or the discovery that the moon is made of cream cheese. Why?
- Have students name some things that were revelations to them in the past.

elicit

Human everyday sounds sometimes get a response from the animal kingdom. You might also say that the sounds elicit a response. If you elicit a response from a person or animal, you cause it by doing or saying something.

- Ask students which has elicited a response, the doorbell which brings a person to the door or a knock on the door which goes unheard and unanswered. Explain.
- Have students name some actions and the responses that those actions might elicit.

Summer Days

In this excerpt from *Charlotte's Web*, sweet summer days come to life as the animals on the Zuckerman farm wait eagerly for the goslings to hatch.

Vocabulary

Words From the Story

These words appear in blue in the story. Explain these words after the story is read.

hoist	**scruples**
jubilee	**nudge**
unremitting	

Words About the Story

Explain these words after the story is read, using context from the story.

tranquil	**eccentric**
rejuvenate	

Getting Ready for the Read-Aloud

Show students the picture on page 33 and read the title aloud. Explain that the rat is holding one of the geese's eggs. Have them notice the expression on the rat's face and tell what they think is happening in the picture.

Explain to students that "Summer Days" is an excerpt from a book called *Charlotte's Web.* Tell them that, in this story, the animals speak to each other. Then explain that they live in a barn together and learn to get along as a community.

There are some words and phrases in the story that may be new to students. You might wish to briefly explain these words and phrases as you come to them: *swathes,* strips; *timothy,* a kind of hay; *interlude,* a period of time; *loaded with nectar,* full of a thick, sweet juice; *lair,* hiding place.

Summer Days

from
Charlotte's Web

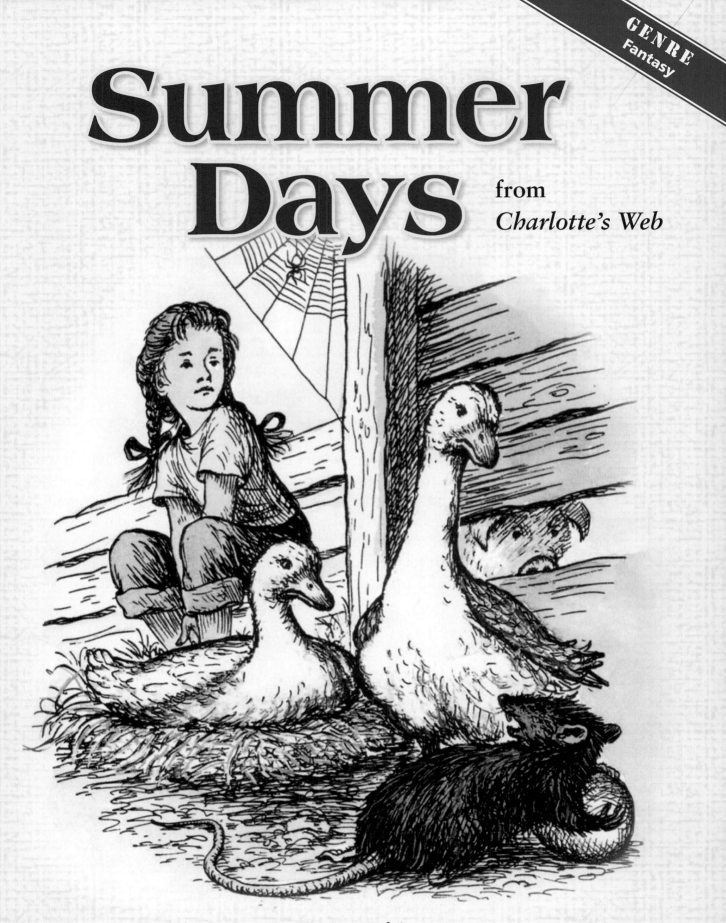

By E. B. White
Illustrated by Garth Williams

Bringing the Story to Life

Read the descriptive passage that opens the story in an awed tone. Read the rest of the story by infusing each character's voice with an inflection that matches their nature. For example, try using a proud and dignified voice for the mother goose, a sneaky voice for Templeton the rat, an authoritative voice for Charlotte, etc. Phrases such as "stink bomb" and "junky old rotten egg" should be read exuberantly.

A horse-drawn lawn mower? This was a long time ago, wasn't it?

Many things come in sevens: there are seven days in the week, seven dwarves, and seven continents. One beautiful summer day, seven goslings hatch on Mr. Zuckerman's farm. There to witness the happy breakthrough are Fern, who is Mr. Zuckerman's daughter and Avery's sister; Charlotte, the wise and mysterious spider; and Wilbur, the pig. According to Charlotte, seven is a lucky number, but does Templeton the rat agree?

The early summer days on a farm are the happiest and fairest days of the year. Lilacs bloom and make the air sweet, and then fade. Apple blossoms come with the lilacs, and the bees visit around among the apple trees. The days grow warm and soft. School ends, and children have time to play and to fish for trouts in the brook. Avery often brought a trout home in his pocket, warm and stiff and ready to be fried for supper.

Now that school was over, Fern visited the barn almost every day, to sit quietly on her stool. The animals treated her as an equal. The sheep lay calmly at her feet.

Around the first of July, the work horses were hitched to the mowing machine, and Mr. Zuckerman climbed into the seat and drove into the field.

All morning you could hear the rattle of the machine as it went round and round, while the tall grass fell down behind the cutter bar in long green swathes. Next day, if there was no thunder shower, all hands would help rake and pitch and load, and the hay would be hauled to the barn in the high hay wagon, with Fern and Avery riding at the top of the load.

Then the hay would be **hoisted**, sweet and warm, into the big loft, until the whole barn seemed like a wonderful bed of timothy and clover. It was fine to jump in, and perfect to hide in. And sometimes Avery would find a little grass snake in the hay, and would add it to the other things in his pocket.

Early summer days are a **jubilee** time for birds. In the fields, around the house, in the barn, in the woods, in the swamp—everywhere love and songs and nests and eggs. From the edge of the woods, the white-throated sparrow (which must come all the way from Boston) calls, "Oh, Peabody, Peabody, Peabody!" On an apple bough, the phoebe teeters and wags its tail and says, "Phoebe, phoe-bee!" The song sparrow, who knows how brief and lovely life is, says, "Sweet, sweet, sweet interlude; sweet, sweet, sweet interlude." If you enter the barn, the swallows swoop down from their nests and scold. "Cheeky, cheeky!" they say.

In early summer there are plenty of things for a child to eat and drink and suck and chew. Dandelion stems are full of milk, clover heads are loaded with nectar, the refrigerator is full of ice-cold drinks. Everywhere you look is life; even the little ball of spit on the weed stalk, if you poke it apart, has a green worm inside it.

> That must be why the goslings are going to be born in the summer.

And on the under side of the leaf of the potato vine are the bright orange eggs of the potato bug.

It was on a day in early summer that the goose eggs hatched. This was an important event in the barn cellar. Fern was there, sitting on her stool, when it happened.

Except for the goose herself, Charlotte was the first to know that the goslings had at last arrived. The goose knew a day in advance that they were coming—she could hear their weak voices calling from inside the egg. She knew that they were in a desperately cramped position inside the shell and were most anxious to break through and get out. So she sat quite still, and talked less than usual.

> Why was the mother goose still and quiet?

When the first gosling poked its grey-green head through the goose's feathers and looked around, Charlotte spied it and made the announcement.

"I am sure," she said, "that every one of us here will be gratified to learn that after four weeks of **unremitting** effort and patience on the part of our friend the goose, she now has something to show for it. The goslings have arrived. May I offer my sincere congratulations!"

"Thank you, thank you, thank you!" said the goose, nodding and bowing shamelessly.

"Thank you," said the gander.

"Congratulations!" shouted Wilbur. "How many goslings are there? I can only see one."

"There are seven," said the goose.

"Fine!" said Charlotte. "Seven is a lucky number."

"Luck had nothing to do with this," said the goose. "It was good management and hard work."

At this point, Templeton showed his nose from his hiding place under Wilbur's trough. He glanced at Fern, then crept cautiously toward the goose, keeping close to the wall. Everyone watched him, for he was not well liked, not trusted.

"Look," he began in his sharp voice, "you say you have seven goslings. There were eight eggs. What happened to the other egg? Why didn't it hatch?"

"It's a dud, I guess," said the goose.

"What are you going to do with it?" continued Templeton, his little round beady eyes fixed on the goose.

"You can have it," replied the goose. "Roll it away and add it to that nasty collection of yours." (Templeton had a habit of picking up unusual objects around the farm and storing them in his home. He saved everything.)

"Certainly-ertainly-ertainly," said the gander. "You may have the egg. But I'll tell you one thing, Templeton, if I ever catch you poking-oking-oking your ugly nose around our goslings, I'll give you the worst pounding a rat ever took."

And the gander opened his strong wings and beat the air with them to show his power. He was strong and brave, but the truth is, both the goose and the gander were worried about Templeton. And with good reason. The rat had no morals, no conscience, no **scruples**, no consideration, no decency, no milk of rodent kindness, no compunctions, no higher feeling, no friendliness, no anything. He would kill a gosling if he could get away with it—the goose knew that. Everybody knew it.

With her broad bill the goose pushed the unhatched egg out of the nest, and the entire company watched in disgust while the rat rolled it away. Even Wilbur, who could eat almost anything, was appalled. "Imagine wanting a junky old rotten egg!" he muttered.

"A rat is a rat," said Charlotte. She laughed a tinkling little laugh. "But, my friends, if that ancient egg ever breaks, this barn will be untenable."

"What's that mean?" asked Wilbur.

"It means nobody will be able to live here on account of the smell. A rotten egg is a regular stink bomb."

"I won't break it," snarled Templeton. "I know what I'm doing. I handle stuff like this all the time."

He disappeared into his tunnel, pushing the goose egg in front of him. He pushed and **nudged** till he succeeded in rolling it to his lair under the trough.

That afternoon, when the wind had died down and the barnyard was quiet and warm, the grey goose led her seven goslings off the nest and out into the world. Mr. Zuckerman spied them when he came with Wilbur's supper.

"Well, hello there!" he said, smiling all over. "Let's see . . . one, two, three, four, five, six, seven. Seven baby geese. Now isn't that lovely!"

Why do the goose and the gander let Templeton have the egg?

Talking About the Story

Have students tell how summer days are full of life. Then ask them if they think that both Templeton and the geese get what they want.

Ask students to tell about a special summer memory.

Words From the Story

hoist

In the story, the farm hands hoist hay into the barn loft. If you hoist something heavy, you pull it or lift it up.

- Ask students what they might have to hoist, a backpack or the wind. Explain your answer.
- Have students use body language to show how they would hoist something really heavy.

jubilee

In the story, the author describes summer days as a jubilee time for birds. A jubilee is a celebration to mark a special anniversary of an event.

- Ask students which is a jubilee, a Fourth of July festival at a city park or dinner at home with your family. Explain why.
- Have students tell of a recent jubilee in their family.

unremitting

In the story, the goose is unremitting in her patience as she waits for the goslings to hatch. If something is unremitting, it goes on and on without stopping.

- Ask which is unremitting, rain or the beating of your heart. Why do you think so?
- Have students give an example of something that is unremitting.

scruples

The author writes that Templeton the rat has no scruples. Someone's scruples are their ideas about what is fair, honest, and right.

- Ask who has scruples, a person who keeps someone's lost camera or a person who returns someone's lost camera. Explain.
- Have students tell of a person who they think has scruples.

nudge

Templeton nudges the egg to his lair. If you nudge someone or something, you give them a gentle push, usually with an elbow.

- Ask students when you might be nudged, when you are falling asleep in class or when you are paying attention in class. Why?
- Have students show how they might nudge someone.

Words About the Story

tranquil

In the story, summer days are described as being relaxing. You could say that they are tranquil. If something or someone is tranquil, they are calm and peaceful.

- Ask students what might make them feel tranquil, hearing a loud crash or hearing a soft whisper. Why?
- Have students describe a time when they felt very tranquil.

rejuvenate

Summer days are full of life and can make you feel young again. In other words, they can rejuvenate you. If something rejuvenates you, it makes you feel young or fresh again.

- Ask what might rejuvenate you, playing in the sprinkler on a hot day or wearing a sweater on a hot day. Explain your answer.
- Have students go from looking old and tired to looking rejuvenated.

eccentric

When Templeton takes away the rotten, old egg, everyone thinks that he is strange. Another way to say that is that they think he is eccentric. An eccentric person does or says things that other people think are strange.

- Ask who is eccentric, a man who wears a soup bowl on his head or a man who drives a truck. Why do you think so?
- Have students show how they might look as an eccentric person.

A Concert to Remember

This article talks about singer Marian Anderson and her concert at the Lincoln Memorial, a victory for African Americans and a turning point in race relations.

Vocabulary

Words From the Story

These words appear in blue in the story. Explain these words after the story is read.

acclaim	furor
curt	endow
imply	

Words About the Story

Explain these words after the story is read, using context from the story.

hamper	enthralled
qualm	

Getting Ready for the Read-Aloud

Show students the picture of Marian Anderson on page 41 and read the title aloud. Explain that Anderson was a talented African-American singer. Have students notice how she looks as though she is remembering something.

Explain that this is a nonfiction story that tells how Marian Anderson and others in our country responded when she was not allowed to perform at a concert hall. Then tell students that the story takes place in the 1930s and that, at that time, there were many places where African Americans were not allowed because of their skin color. Ask students to listen for moments in the story where other people help Marian's voice to be heard.

Explain the following phrases as they occur in the story: *decried*, harshly criticized; *contralto*, woman singer with a low voice; *reflecting pool*, a pool of still water designed to mirror the Washington Monument; *ears glued to the radio*, listening very closely; *mass of humanity*, huge group of people; *spiritual*, a traditional religious song.

A Concert to Remember

from *Marian Anderson:*
Singer and Humanitarian

By Andrea Broadwater

Bringing the Story to Life

Why did Marian's manager think it was time for her to sing in the United States' capital?

Marian Anderson was born in 1897 in Philadelphia, Pennsylvania. Early in her singing career, she was recognized for her rich and velvety voice. Marian believed that no one should prevent her from singing because she was an African American, even if it sparked national protests.

By 1939, Marian Anderson had performed to high **acclaim** in cities all over the world—London, Paris, Moscow, Buenos Aires, New York. Her manager, Sol Hurok, in conjunction with Howard University, understandably thought that the time had come for a major performance in the capital of her own country. What should have been a routine request to reserve Constitution Hall in Washington, D.C., evolved into an event that challenged the very ideals and laws of the United States.

The music department of Howard University applied to the Constitution Hall, to reserve the hall for April 9, 1939, for Anderson's concert. However, a clause in the rental contract prohibited the presentation of African-American artists. The reply was **curt** and to the point: "The hall is not available for a concert by Miss Anderson."

Constitution Hall was owned, tax free, by the Daughters of the American Revolution (DAR), an organization of women with white ancestors who had served in the American Revolutionary War. When news spread of the ban on an appearance by Marian Anderson, telegrams and phone calls of protest flooded the DAR office. A group of musicians and clergy sent a telegram stating:

> We read with astonishment the reports in the press that the Daughters of the American Revolution have refused the use of Constitution Hall to Marian Anderson. . . .[It] places your organization . . . in the camp of those who today seek to destroy democracy, justice and liberty.

> Do you think that more people will try to help Marian?

News articles and editorials decried the treatment of Anderson. Then, one protest rang out the loudest of them all across the nation. On February 27, 1939, the DAR received a resignation in protest from its most prominent member—First Lady Eleanor Roosevelt. In her "My Day" column, published in New York's *World-Telegram*, she wrote: "I belong to an organization in which I can do no active work. They have taken an action which has been widely talked of in the press. To remain as a member **implies** approval of that action, and therefore I am resigning."

> Why did Eleanor Roosevelt decide to quit this organization?

The story made the national headlines. Although Mrs. Roosevelt did not name the organization, it was clearly understood that she had resigned from the Daughters of the American Revolution.

Sol Hurok was not upset by the controversy. He saw the ban as an opportunity to enlighten the public on what had been happening over the years. Hurok saw the **furor** as a culmination of the many injustices Anderson had endured in her career. He stated: "After the constantly recurring offenses . . . it was almost a relief when the Daughters of the American Revolution presented Marian's friends with an issue big enough to bring out into the open."

Can you believe things like this had happened to Marian Anderson before?

Hurok announced that Marian Anderson would sing on the steps of the Lincoln Memorial on Easter Sunday, April 9, 1939.

The day of the Lincoln Memorial concert was quickly approaching, and Anderson was undecided about going through with it. For a concert of hers to be such a sensational and political event was wholly contrary to her beliefs. Anderson believed that art should not be used for political purposes. The artistry itself should speak for the equality of the races. Still, Anderson realized that the whole incident had become something much bigger than just her singing in a concert hall. She later stated, "I could see that my significance as an individual was small in this affair. I had become, whether I liked it or not, a symbol, representing my people." When the day arrived, her professionalism took over, and she was ready to take her place in the national spotlight.

Why did Marian decide to perform?

On Easter Sunday, April 9, 1939, a brisk wind swirled around the more than seventy-five thousand people, black and white, who gathered at the foot of the Lincoln Memorial to hear the great contralto.

Secretary of the Interior Harold Ickes introduced Anderson to the crowd, which stretched from the monument, along the banks of the reflecting pool, to the mound of the Washington Monument. Also listening to his words were millions of people all over the nation with their ears glued to the radio. In his speech, Ickes declared, "Genius draws no color line. She has **endowed** Marian Anderson with such a voice as lifts any individual above his fellows, as is a matter of exultant pride to any race."

Then, before the huge crowd charged with anticipation, Anderson appeared between the towering marble columns. Dressed in a long black velvet dress and mink coat around her shoulders, she strode toward the cluster of microphones. Before the breathtaking view of the mass of humanity, Anderson began. "America" was first. Among the other selections were "O Mio Fernando," "Ave Maria," and the spiritual "My Soul Is Anchored in the Lord." Each song received a burst of applause. She sang her final number, the spiritual "Nobody Knows the Trouble I've Seen," in her usual posture, with her eyes closed and hands clasped. The spiritual ended to thunderous applause.

Overwhelmed by the enormous support shown to her that day, Anderson told the crowd, "I can't tell you what you have done for me today. I thank you from the bottom of my heart again and again."

How do you think Marian felt after being introduced like that?

Talking About the Story

Have students tell why Marian was thanking the crowd and how they think Marian showed courage.

Ask students to talk about a time when they or someone else had to be courageous.

Vocabulary in Action

Words From the Story

acclaim

In the story, Anderson received acclaim for her singing in many places. If you earn acclaim, you are getting public praise for something you have done.

- Ask who would receive acclaim, a firefighter who saves a child or someone who tells a lie. Explain why.
- Have students tell of a time when they or someone they know received acclaim.

curt

The reply from the people at Constitution Hall was curt. If you say something in a curt manner, you say it in a short, somewhat rude way.

- Ask students who is being curt, someone who asks you if you could please keep the noise down or someone who yells, "Be quiet!" Why do you think so?
- Have students tell about a time when someone was curt with them.

imply

Eleanor Roosevelt did not want to stay a member of the DAR because doing so would have implied that she agreed with their actions. If you imply something, you don't say it directly, but you let others think that is what you mean.

- Ask which is an example of implying something, telling someone that you hate milk or pushing a glass of milk away. Explain.
- Have students imply that they are bored by checking their watches (or by pretending to, if they do not wear one) and sighing.

furor

When Anderson was not allowed to reserve Constitution Hall, it created a furor. A furor is a very angry and excited reaction that people have to something.

- Ask what might cause a furor, millions of parents all trying to buy the same toy for their child or someone receiving a get-well note from a friend. Why?
- Have students make a statement about the school cafeteria that might cause a furor.

endow

In the story, Anderson was endowed with a beautiful singing voice. If someone is endowed with some special quality or ability, they have it naturally.

- Ask students who has an endowed talent, someone who loves to write and has always been good at it or someone who has a hard time finding the right words to write. Explain your answer.
- Have students talk about other people who have been endowed with special talents.

Words About the Story

hamper

In the story, the DAR made it difficult for Marian Anderson to sing in Washington, D.C. In other words, they hampered her efforts. If someone or something hampers you, they make it difficult for you to do what you are trying to do.

- Ask what might hamper your efforts to get home today, your school bus driving you to your neighborhood or your school bus driving you to Mexico. Explain why.
- Have students hamper their ability to hear by placing their hands over their ears.

qualm

Anderson had second thoughts about singing on the steps at the Lincoln Memorial. You could say that she had qualms. If you have qualms about something, you are worried that it may be wrong in some way.

- Ask which situation would give you qualms, deciding whether or not to accept praise for someone else's idea or deciding whether or not to do a crossword puzzle. Why?
- Have students tell about a time when they had qualms about something.

enthralled

Anderson's voice held everyone's attention. Another way to say that is that her voice enthralled everyone. If you are enthralled by something, it completely holds your attention because it is so interesting or exciting.

- Ask students what is more likely to enthrall them, an incredible dancer or an eraser. Explain your answer.
- Have students take turns looking as though they are enthralled with what someone is saying.

Tom Paints the Fence

In this excerpt from *The Adventures of Tom Sawyer*, Tom decides there are better ways to spend his Saturday than whitewashing his aunt's fence.

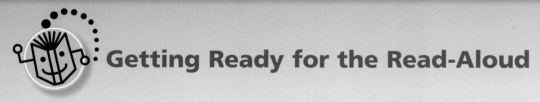

Vocabulary

Words From the Story

These words appear in blue in the story. Explain these words after the story is read.

melancholy	absorbed
insignificant	dilapidated

Words About the Story

Explain these words after the story is read, using context from the story.

manipulate	precocious
pompous	scheme

Getting Ready for the Read-Aloud

Show students the picture on page 49 and read the title aloud. Explain to them that the boy with the paintbrush is "whitewashing" the fence. Then have them notice the boy who is sitting down and the expression on his face. Ask them to tell what they think is happening in the picture.

Explain to students that "Tom Paints the Fence" is an excerpt from a book called *The Adventures of Tom Sawyer*. Tell them that the story is set in Hannibal, Missouri, a town along the Mississippi River, during the 1800s. The people of that time had very few machines and had to do most jobs without the help of technology.

The following terms can be briefly explained as you come to them: *music issued at the lips*, person would sing aloud; *delicious expeditions*, adventures; *straitened means*, small amount of money; *hove in sight*, moved into view ("hove" usually refers to the act of moving a ship in a certain direction); *up a stump*, to not know what to say or think; *alacrity*, eagerness; *slaughter of more innocents*, to easily trick more people; *decanter*, fancy, glass bottle; *obliged*, required.

Tom Paints the Fence

from
The Adventures of Tom Sawyer
By Mark Twain

Illustrated by
Joel Spector

Bringing the Story to Life

Read the story dramatically, with a sly, ironic edge. In the first paragraph, let listeners hear your reverence for the exalted beauty of the Saturday morning. Employ an empathetic tone in the next two paragraphs until "inspiration burst[s] upon" Tom. Tom should not seem transparent as you read his lines, but students should be able to detect something disingenuous in your tone when he speaks.

Why is Tom discouraged?

Saturday morning was come, and all the summer world was bright and fresh, and brimming with life. There was a song in every heart; and if the heart was young the music issued at the lips. There was cheer in every face and a spring in every step. The locust-trees were in bloom and the fragrance of the blossoms filled the air. Cardiff Hill, beyond the village and above it, was green with vegetation and it lay just far enough away to seem a Delectable Land, dreamy, reposeful, and inviting.

Tom appeared on the sidewalk with a bucket of whitewash and a long-handled brush. He surveyed the fence, and all gladness left him and a deep **melancholy** settled down upon his spirit. Thirty yards of board fence nine feet high. Life to him seemed hollow, and existence but a burden. Sighing, he dipped his brush and passed it along the topmost plank; repeated the operation; did it again; compared the **insignificant** whitewashed streak with the far-reaching continent of unwhitewashed fence, and sat down on a tree-box discouraged.

He began to think of the fun he had planned for this day, and his sorrows multiplied. Soon the free boys would come tripping along on all sorts of delicious expeditions, and they would make a world of fun of him for having to work—the very thought of it burnt him like fire. He got out his worldly wealth and examined it—bits of toys, marbles, and trash; enough to buy an exchange of *work*, maybe, but not half enough to buy so much as half an hour of pure freedom. So he returned his straitened means to his pocket, and gave up the idea of trying to buy the boys. At this dark and hopeless moment an inspiration burst upon him! Nothing less than a great, magnificent inspiration.

What do you think Tom is going to do?

He took up his brush and went tranquilly to work. His friend Ben Rogers hove in sight presently—the very boy, of all boys, whose ridicule he had been dreading. Ben's gait was the hop-skip-and-jump—proof enough that his heart was light and his anticipations high. He was eating an apple, and giving a long, melodious whoop, at intervals, followed by a deep-toned ding-dong-dong, ding-dong-dong, for he was personating a steamboat.

Tom went on whitewashing—paid no attention to the steamboat. Ben stared a moment and then said: "Hi-*yi*! *You're* up a stump, ain't you!"

No answer. Tom surveyed his last touch with the eye of an artist, then he gave his brush another gentle sweep and surveyed the result, as before. Ben ranged up alongside of him. Tom's mouth watered for the apple, but he stuck to his work. Ben said:

"Hello, old chap, you got to work, hey?"

Tom wheeled suddenly and said:

"Why, it's you, Ben! I warn't noticing."

"Say—I'm going in a-swimming, I am. Don't you wish you could? But of course you'd druther *work*—wouldn't you? Course you would!"

It sounds like Ben is making fun of Tom!

Tom contemplated the boy a bit, and said:

"What do you call work?"

"Why, ain't *that* work?"

Tom resumed his whitewashing, and answered carelessly:

"Well, maybe it is, and maybe it ain't. All I know, is, it suits Tom Sawyer."

"Oh come, now, you don't mean to let on that you *like* it?"

The brush continued to move.

"Like it? Well, I don't see why I oughtn't to like it. Does a boy get a chance to whitewash a fence every day?"

Do you think Tom's attitude is going to change Ben's mind?

That put the thing in a new light. Ben stopped nibbling his apple. Tom swept his brush daintily back and forth—stepped back to note the effect—added a touch here and there—criticized the effect again—Ben watching every move and getting more and more interested, more and more **absorbed**. Presently he said:

"Say, Tom, let *me* whitewash a little."

Why does Ben want to whitewash the fence?

Tom considered, was about to consent; but he altered his mind:

"No—no—I reckon it wouldn't hardly do, Ben. You see, Aunt Polly's awful particular about this fence—right here on the street, you know—but if it was the back fence I wouldn't mind and *she* wouldn't. Yes, she's awful particular about this fence; it's got to be done very careful; I reckon there ain't one boy in a thousand, maybe two thousand, that can do it the way it's got to be done."

"No—is that so? Oh come, now—lemme just try. Only just a little—I'd let *you*, if you was me, Tom."

"Ben, I'd like to, honest, but Aunt Polly—well, Jim wanted to do it, but she wouldn't let him; Sid wanted to do it, and she wouldn't let Sid. Now don't you see how I'm fixed? If you was to tackle this fence and anything was to happen to it—"

Why do you think Tom is telling this to Ben?

"Oh, shucks, I'll be just as careful. Now lemme try. Say—I'll give you the core of my apple."

"Well, here—No, Ben, now don't. I'm afeard—"

"I'll give you *all* of it!"

Tom gave up the brush with reluctance in his face, but alacrity in his heart. And while the late steamer worked and sweated in the sun, the retired artist sat on a barrel in the shade close by, dangled his legs, munched his apple, and planned the slaughter of more innocents.

So what was Tom's plan? Did it work?

There was no lack of material; boys happened along every little while; they came to jeer, but remained to whitewash. By the time Ben was tuckered out, Tom had traded the next chance to Billy Fisher for a kite, in good repair; and when he played out, Johnny Miller bought in for a dead rat and a string to swing it with—and so on, and so on, hour after hour.

And when the middle of the afternoon came, from being a poor poverty-stricken boy in the morning, Tom was literally rolling in wealth. He had besides the things before mentioned, twelve marbles, part of a mouth harp, a piece of blue bottle-glass to look through, a spool cannon, a key that wouldn't unlock anything, a fragment of chalk, a glass stopper of a decanter, a tin soldier, a couple of tadpoles, six fire-crackers, a kitten with only one eye, a brass doorknob, a dog-collar—but no dog—the handle of a knife, four pieces of orange-peel, and a **dilapidated** old window frame.

He had had a nice, good, idle time all the while—plenty of company—and the fence had three coats of whitewash on it! If he hadn't run out of whitewash he would have bankrupted every boy in the village.

Tom said to himself that it was not such a hollow world, after all. He had discovered a great law of human action, without knowing it—namely, that in order to make a man or a boy covet a thing, it is only necessary to make the thing difficult to attain. If he had been a great and wise philosopher, like the writer of this story, he would now have comprehended that Work consists of whatever a body is *obliged* to do, and that Play consists of whatever a body is not obliged to do.

Talking About the Story

Have students summarize what happened in the story. How did Tom manage to trick so many boys into doing his work?

Ask students to listen closely as you read the last paragraph again. Then ask students if they agree or disagree and have them tell what they think the difference is between work and play.

Words From the Story

melancholy

In the story, Tom is melancholy because he has to paint the fence. If you feel or look melancholy, you feel or look very sad.

- Ask students what might make them feel melancholy, being greeted by a friend or being ignored by a friend. Explain why.
- Have students take turns looking melancholy.

insignificant

The part of the fence that Tom paints looks insignificant when compared with the part that is still unpainted. If something is insignificant, it is unimportant, usually because it is very small.

- Ask which is an insignificant amount of money, one cent or twenty dollars. Explain.
- Have students talk about something they thought was important that turned out to be insignificant.

absorbed

Ben gets absorbed in watching Tom whitewash the fence. If you are absorbed in something, you are so interested in it that it takes all your attention.

- Ask students what they might get absorbed in, an interesting story or a boring speech. Why do you think so?
- Have students take turns acting absorbed in one of their textbooks.

dilapidated

In the story, Tom receives a dilapidated window frame. Something that is dilapidated is old and in bad condition.

- Ask students which is dilapidated, a shiny, new scooter or an old house with broken windows and cobwebs. Explain your answer.
- Have students describe something they have seen that looks dilapidated.

Words About the Story

manipulate

Tom tricks the boys into doing his work. Another way to say that is that he manipulates them into doing his work. If you manipulate someone, you use skill to unfairly force or convince them to do what you want.

- Ask who is manipulating someone, a girl who gets her parents to buy her expensive clothes by crying or a girl who gets a phone call from her parents. Why do you think so?

- Have students talk about a time when they tried to manipulate their parents into letting them stay up later.

pompous

Tom acts as though he's the only person good enough to whitewash the fence. In other words, he acts pompous. A pompous person acts or speaks in a way that shows they think they're more important than they really are.

- Ask who might be considered pompous, someone who won't answer you unless you call them "sir" or a person planting a garden. Explain.

- Have students practice acting in a pompous way.

precocious

In the story, Tom is surprisingly good at getting other people to do his work for him. Another way to say that is that his behavior is precocious. A precocious child is very smart, mature, or good at something in a way you would only expect an adult to be.

- Ask students who would be precocious, a three-year-old child who could do advanced math or a baby who could suck her thumb. Why?

- Have students talk about someone they think is precocious in some way.

scheme

Tom comes up with a clever plan to get out of whitewashing the fence. In other words, he has a scheme to get out of whitewashing the fence. A scheme is someone's plan for achieving a goal.

- Ask who might come up with a scheme, someone who is giving money to the poor or someone who wants to get rich quickly. Explain why.

- Have students think of a clever scheme to get something they want.

GEOFFREY PYKE'S COOL IDEA

Geoffrey Pyke invented a new way to make the aircraft carrier *Habbakuk* during World War II using a very unusual combination of materials.

Vocabulary

Words From the Story

These words appear in blue in the story. Explain these words after the story is read.

ease   undertaking

propose   penetrate

portable

Words About the Story

Explain these words after the story is read, using context from the story.

durable   ingenious

indebted

Getting Ready for the Read-Aloud

Show students the picture on page 58 and read the title aloud. Have students note that the man pictured, Geoffrey Pyke, is looking at an ice cube. Ask what ideas he might have about ice and how those ideas might help the war effort.

Explain that this story takes place during World War II. Many countries, including the United States, Great Britain, and Germany, fought on the ocean, where dropping torpedoes on enemy ships was an important part of fighting the war. Explain that torpedoes are special bombs designed to blow up ships.

There are some words and phrases in the story that may be new to students. Briefly explain these expressions as you come to them: *aircraft carrier,* a huge boat whose deck is an aiplane runway; *H.M.S.,* an abbreviation before the names of English ships, meaning "Her/His Majesty's Ship"; *7 knots,* 7 nautical miles per hour, a little more than 8 miles an hour; *English Channel,* the narrow strip of water between England and France; *Normandy,* an area on the north coast of France.

GEOFFREY PYKE'S COOL IDEA

By Louise Gruppen

Illustrated by Jan Adkins

Keep your delivery light and fun. Emphasize the plot elements and allow the facts to highlight themselves. Use a dramatic voice to describe the torpedo attacks and battles.

Returning from his bombing mission, the World War II fighter pilot brought his plane down with **ease** onto the aircraft carrier H.M.S. *Habbakuk.* "I can't believe I'm landing this plane on a ship made of ice," he mumbled to himself.

Sound like a scene from a science fiction movie? Actually, this ship was the dream of Geoffrey Nathaniel Pyke. He believed it was possible to build an aircraft carrier from a mixture of ice and wood pulp. Why would he **propose** such a strange idea?

Aircraft carriers played an essential role in World War II. They acted as **portable** airports, allowing planes to take off and land on a ship in the middle of the ocean. Two of the aircraft carriers used in World War II, the *Lexington* and the *Saratoga,* could carry 83 planes each. Some of these planes defended the aircraft carrier, while others dropped bombs or torpedoes on enemy targets. Without the aircraft carriers, these planes would have had to take off from land to fight battles at sea. Therefore, they would have to fly many more hours and carry a lot more fuel and fewer bombs.

Why are the aircraft carriers important?

Because the carriers were so important in battle, they were a prime target for enemy torpedoes. When they were struck, fires and explosions resulted, and the ships often sank. Within a ten-month period in 1942, four United States Navy aircraft carriers were sunk. Replacing these ships was an expensive and lengthy **undertaking**.

Great Britain was experiencing the same problems. Geoffrey Pyke, an English inventor, was determined to find a solution. During World War II, Pyke was an adviser to Lord Louis Mountbatten, a member of the Chief of Combined Operations, which planned strategies for the war. Concerned about the number of aircraft carriers being sunk, Pyke proposed a new way of making them out of a mixture of wood pulp and ice.

This mixture was first called piccolite, and later called pykrete, after Pyke.

Pyke began by mixing water with a small amount of tiny woodchips, then freezing this substance into small blocks. A number of tests proved that the material was incredibly strong. In one test, an official tried to smash a small block of pykrete with a hammer, but the hammer bounced off the block, hurting the official's arm in the process. During another test, a researcher fired one bullet at a block of pykrete and another one at a block of wood. The bullet **penetrated** the wood 25 inches but only penetrated the pykrete 6.5 inches. In another test, someone poured boiling water over a block of pykrete, but it did not melt.

Pyke was convinced that building aircraft carriers out of pykrete would solve several problems. Torpedoes would only penetrate the ships a short distance, and the damage could be repaired. Therefore, the carriers could get very close to enemy ships. They would also be unsinkable. Just as ice floats because it is less dense than water, pykrete would float because it is even less dense than ice. Pyke believed these ships would be indestructible.

Pyke drew up plans to build a 2,000-foot-long ship that would hold 300 planes. The outside would be covered with wood, followed by insulation, then pykrete. The hull, or walls of the ship, would be 40 feet thick. A complicated refrigeration system would keep the ship at the necessary temperature to prevent thawing. The trade-off of building a ship so large was a much slower speed. The carrier would only move at 7 knots, compared to 35 knots of the 890-foot-long *Lexington* and the *Saratoga*. Since Pyke's ship would not sustain great damage from enemy ships, the slower speed was not a problem.

After he proposed his idea, Pyke won the approval of Lord Mountbatten and Winston Churchill, the Prime Minister of England. Further tests were done in Canada, where slabs of pykrete were bombed and torpedoed, with little resulting damage.

Finally, a 60-foot model of the ship was built on Patricia Lake in Jasper, Ontario, in 1943. It stayed afloat and did not melt all summer.

The ship was named the *Habbakuk*. Isn't that an odd name?

Although some people were supportive of Pyke's plan, others thought it would never work. Some scientists were concerned that the motors on the *Habbakuk* would create so much heat that the ship would melt. There was also concern about the labor and expense needed to build it. Other problems were considered as well.

The *Habbakuk* would have been limited to certain areas because some places, like the English Channel, were too shallow. Plans called for keeping the carrier in the North Atlantic, particularly to aid in the invasion of France. It took many months to try to convince the right people to build this ship. In the meantime, plans for the location of the invasion of France had changed, and the Allies decided to launch air attacks from England to the beaches of Normandy. It was decided that the *Habbakuk* was no longer needed, so it was never built.

Was the project a failure? No. Pyke's idea of using ice as a building material has led to other projects, such as constructing runways out of ice and twigs in northern Canada and highways out of similar material in northern Siberia.

Clearly, it took a lot of courage and persistence for Geoffrey Pyke to promote such a new and strange invention, and he is still known for his very "cool idea."

Talking About the Story

Have students summarize what happened in the article and tell what they learned.

Ask students if they think Pyke's idea was a success. What do they think it means for an idea to be a success?

Vocabulary in Action

Words From the Story

ease

In the story, the pilot brought his plane onto the aircraft carrier with ease. If you do something with ease, it's not hard for you to do it.

- Ask students which can be done with ease, throwing a shoe or throwing a house. Why do you think so?
- Have students take turns describing things they can do with ease.

propose

Pyke proposed the unusual idea of using ice to build a boat. If you propose a plan or idea, you suggest it.

- Ask who is proposing something, the student who stares out the window at the sunny day or the student who tries to convince the teacher to teach the class outside in the sun. Why?
- Ask students to propose something.

portable

In the story, aircraft carriers are described as portable airports. If something is portable, it is easy to move or carry.

- Ask students which is portable, a lake or a cup of water. Explain your answer.
- Have students give examples of things that are portable.

undertaking

Replacing lost aircraft carriers is an expensive undertaking. If you undertake a large or difficult task, you say that you will do it.

- Ask students which is an undertaking, building a fancy doll house or playing with dolls. Why is that?
- Have students describe how they would feel if asked to undertake the job of cleaning the entire school, top to bottom.

penetrate

In the story, the bullets didn't penetrate very far into the pykrete. Something that penetrates something else goes into it or passes through it.

- Ask what can easily penetrate a cork board, a push pin or clear tape. Explain.
- Have students use a pencil to penetrate a piece of paper.

Words About the Story

durable

Pyke invented a very tough, strong material. You could say it was a durable material. If something is durable, it is strong and lasts a long time.

- Ask students which is more durable, a piece of tissue paper or a block of cement. Why?
- Have students think of the most durable material they can. Why did they make this choice?

indebted

Future inventors felt deeply grateful to Pyke for his invention. You could say they felt indebted to Pyke. If you feel indebted to someone, you are so grateful for something they did that you feel you owe them something in return.

- Ask who might feel indebted, someone who has been given a big diamond or someone who has been given a penny. Explain.
- Have students volunteer to describe a time they felt indebted to someone else. Why did they feel this way?

ingenious

Pyke's invention was surprisingly clever and unusual. You could say it was ingenious. Something that is ingenious is very clever and original.

- Ask which is ingenious, a t-shirt made out of cotton or a t-shirt made out of duct-tape. Why do you think so?
- Have students tell about an ingenious idea they have.

The Wisdom of Goats

In this Mexican folktale, a lonely old man and his beloved goats teach a village a lesson in faith and respect.

Vocabulary

Words From the Story

These words appear in blue in the story. Explain these words after the story is read.

nuzzle	**refuge**
trepidation	**grapple**

Words About the Story

Explain these words after the story is read, using context from the story.

ridicule	**countermand**
tempest	**luminous**

Getting Ready for the Read-Aloud

Show students the picture of the old man and his goats on page 65 and read the title aloud. Then tell them that the goats belong to the old man. Have students notice the expression on the old man's face. Then ask them if they can guess why the old man is smiling.

Explain to students that this story focuses on an old man who is treated like a fool by the people of the nearby village. Then tell them that the goats in this story are actually able to communicate with the old man, but no one believes it. Explain to students that, often, elderly people know more about the world than younger people since they have lived longer and have experienced more things.

The following terms occur in the story: *trough*, a container that holds food or water for animals; *billy*, male goat; *his brow was deeply furrowed*, he was wrinkling his forehead a lot; *stingy*, giving very little; *ruffians*, bullies; *daft*, crazy; *charitable*, judging someone kindly; *root cellar*, underground storage area for potatoes or other vegetables; *regaling*, entertaining or amusing; *strewn*, scattered; *smirk*, mean smile.

The Wisdom of Goats

By Sandra Clough

Illustrated by Wendy Edelson

Bringing the Story to Life

Long ago and many miles from here, there lived an old man who kept goats. To everyone else, they looked like ordinary goats, but the old man didn't think they were ordinary at all. In fact, he insisted, they were extraordinary.

Sometimes, he said, his goats told him things before they actually happened.

The old man lived by himself, with no wife or children to talk to. The villagers called him the goat man, and when he spoke aloud about the wisdom of his goats, they would say, "Well, what do you expect? He lives all alone, with no one to talk to but those smelly goats. It's no wonder he's so odd!"

Actually most of the folks in that area raised sheep, and they thought goats were remarkably stupid animals. Goats chewed freshly washed clothes right off the line, and they liked to climb onto low-hanging roofs and stick their noses into the wind. Goats, they said, were some of the dumbest creatures God ever put on this earth.

One fine spring morning the old man carried a bucket of corn and carrots into the barnyard, and his goats bounded to meet him as they always did. Their silky beards and pointy ears and tails gave them a comical look, and the sight of them made the old man smile. The goats quickly surrounded him, gently nudging him and his bucket. He assumed they were impatient to eat and said, "Yes, yes, I know I'm late with your breakfast, my pretties, but I have a treat for you: I've mixed raisins with your corn and carrots this morning. It'll be worth the wait, you'll see."

He tried to maneuver through the goats to the trough, but they formed a tight knot. Suspecting something unusual was happening, he stood still and watched as the oldest goat in the herd, a billy he had named Vincent, pushed to the front and stood next to him, **nuzzling** his leg.

What do you think the goats are doing?

The old man reached down and took the goat's bearded face in his hand. "Vincent, my old friend, what's the trouble this morning? Do you have something you want to tell me?"

The goat looked the old man straight in the eye in a way most people have never seen. For several moments the other goats stood very still as the old man and Vincent stayed like that, nose to nose. All was silent except for a decidedly ungoatlike purring that came from the back of Vincent's throat.

Then the spell broke.

The old man no longer smiled. His brow was deeply furrowed, and he took a weary breath, then slowly let it out as he straightened. He walked forward through the opening the goats now gave him and emptied his bucket into the trough.

He was very sorry he'd been so stingy with the raisins.

When he got back to the dilapidated little farmhouse that had been his home since the day he was born, the old man slumped into his rocker. Birds chirped merrily in trees just beyond the door, and flies buzzed impatiently around the screen, waiting for a chance to come inside. But all that went unnoticed by the old man as he pondered what his goat had told him.

> How does the old man feel after what Vincent has told him?

Could it be that Vincent was wrong? Perhaps he's mistaken this time, the old man thought. He's grown old along with me. Perhaps he no longer sees clearly what lies ahead. But the old man was not convinced.

Was it not just a few days ago that Vincent had warned him that hooligans from the village would try to raid his garden? The old man had lain in wait, and when the ruffians approached, he began pounding his largest copper kettle with a soup ladle. He laughed aloud as they dropped their burlap sacks and scattered in all directions.

No, Vincent had not lost his powers.

How has Vincent helped the old man in the past? What powers do you think Vincent has?

Finally when the sun reached its highest point in the sky, the old man pushed himself up out of his seat, having come to a decision. He didn't relish the task before him.

The old man knew the villagers considered him strange, perhaps even a bit daft, they said when they were being charitable. But they were not so charitable when he spoke of the wisdom of his goats. Their winks and smirks cut into the old man's heart and made him dread the occasions when he had to venture off his land, away from his goats.

But he had thought very hard and he knew what must be done.

Awhile later, approaching the village, he felt a mixture of relief and **trepidation**. He was dressed for the chill of early spring, but the day had become unseasonably warm, and the sun beat down hard on him. It would be a relief to step into cool shade, but he didn't dare delay.

He hurried to the village, where he told the mayor that a great storm was coming—the worst they'd ever seen. "We must hurry," he said. "We must go to the church and ring the warning bell so the villagers will gather their children and come to the safety of the sanctuary's stone walls."

Even without mentioning his goats, the old man knew he sounded like a lunatic. The sun shone so brightly, and the sky was so clear; only a madman would think a storm loomed.

The mayor shook his head and smiled with exaggerated tolerance. "Old man, calm yourself. Where did you get such an idea? Not from your goats, I hope! Come, step outside. See how the birds sing and the sun shines. God is smiling on our village today, my friend. Nothing bad will happen to us."

> Why didn't the mayor believe the old man?

Trudging back to his home, the old man felt a great sadness. He had failed.

When he arrived, the sun was still a short distance above the horizon, but now it shone through mottled clouds that dotted the sky. Sunset streaks painted the rickety farmhouse vibrant shades of purple and red. It had never looked so beautiful.

Once inside, he quickly mixed corn and carrots for the goats. But this time when he added the raisins, he didn't skimp.

As he carried the bucket to the barnyard, he saw that the sky had grown dark with clouds, and the air was sharply colder. The goats greeted him impatiently and started eating as soon as he poured their supper. The wind had picked up and made him shiver, but he moved up and down the trough, patting each animal and repeating its name. When he came to Vincent, the old man paused an extra moment, scratching the goat's ears. Then he bent and laid his cheek on the animal's head. "Take care, my old friend," he whispered.

By now the wind was so strong, the old man had to lean into it. Nevertheless he headed to the far end of the barnyard and wrestled with a rusty gate. At last it opened, and nothing stood between the goats and the steep hills and deep ditches of the timberland where he prayed they would find **refuge**.

Then the old man struggled in the direction of the house. Bits of straw and dirt, propelled by the wind, stung his face and blurred his vision.

In the side of a hill, midway between the barnyard and the house, nestled a tiny cave that served as a root cellar. Though it seemed very far away, he was finally there, **grappling** with the door that covered the crevice. He pried it open a few inches, but the wind battered it out of his hands. He tried again and this time managed to hold it long enough to slip inside before it slammed shut.

Crouching in the dark dampness, however, the old man did not rejoice in his safety. Thoughts of the afternoon's failure were nearly as loud in his head as the storm's awful roar.

> Why does the old man feel like he has failed?

What the old man didn't know was that after he left the mayor, such a relatively short time ago, the meanspirited fellow found the story of the goat man's lunacy too entertaining to keep to himself. He meandered the length of the village square in the warm afternoon sun, regaling all who would listen with his comical tale. "You should have heard him! 'Big storm coming, worst we've ever seen!' Wanted me to ring the warning bell and gather everyone into the church. On a beautiful day like this! I think those goats are whispering in his ear again. Ha-ha!" And everywhere he went, his audience joined him in laughter and agreed the old man had lived among goats far too long.

Shortly after that, the first signs of a storm began appearing in the sky. One by one, those who had laughed at the mayor's story recalled the words of the goat man. At last some of the men in the village took matters into their own hands. Against the direct order of the mayor, who still thought the storm would blow over, they rang the warning bell.

Families who had been watching the gathering clouds swarmed into the stone sanctuary. Everyone in the village came—eventually even the mayor. Late into the night, as they listened to the storm rage outside, they spoke in reverent whispers, "He knew! The goat man knew!"

When the storm finally issued its last bellow, it was nearly daybreak. The villagers emerged from their shelter to find homes and shops thrown about like children's toys carelessly tossed aside. But the church had stood strong. Gratefully they accounted for each and every one of their population.

> Do you think the villagers will treat the old man differently now?

The sun was rising in an innocently clear sky when the town's elders went to survey the surrounding farms. They dreaded what they might find. To their amazement, though, they discovered their country neighbors were safe. Having heard the warning bell ring out from the church, the farmers and their families had taken refuge in cellars and caves and ditches. Perhaps they had lost many *things,* but they were safe.

Then the men from the village came to the goat man's farm. Bits of the house were strewn in all directions, and there was no sign of the old man.

They stood for a long time, sadly shaking their heads and saying, "That foolish old man! He knew the storm was coming. Why didn't he stay at the church?"

> Do you think the old man survived the storm?

Just as they were turning away, one of the men heard a faint tapping. It seemed to be coming from behind a heavy door that was pinned against the side of a hill by an uprooted tree.

Could it be? Had that frail old man managed to find shelter?

Frantically the men struggled with the huge tree trunk. Finally they were able to move it a few inches, and they pried the door open. The old man stumbled out.

As his eyes adjusted to the bright light, he looked to the barnyard: there were his goats. Having returned from the safety of the ditches in the timber, they waited impatiently for their breakfast, as though it were any other morning.

The villagers thought the look of relief on the old man's face came from being rescued. They broke into cheers and laughter, and one of them said to him, "Because of your warning, our citizens are safe. We sounded the bell, and the villagers came to the church, and the farmers sought shelter. Everyone is safe—and all because of you. Tell us, old man, how did you know the storm would be so fierce?"

Once more the old man looked to the barnyard. "Why, they told me," he said, surprised anyone had to ask.

The villagers followed his gaze. For a moment they were silent.

Then they laughed again, and one of them said, "Sure, sure, old man!"

But this time their laughter was not confident, and there were no winks or smirks because the men looked at the ground, unable to meet one another's eyes.

Talking About the Story

Have students tell whether the villagers' opinion of the old man and his goats changes. Then have students explain their answers.

Ask students to talk about a time when an elderly person gave them good advice.

Words From the Story

nuzzle

In the story, a goat nuzzles the old man's leg. If a person or animal nuzzles you, they gently rub you with their face to show they like you.

- Ask what animal would most likely nuzzle its owner, a dog or a fish. Explain why.
- Have students talk about a time when an animal nuzzled them.

trepidation

The old man feels trepidation as he walks toward the village to tell the mayor that the storm is on its way. Trepidation is a feeling of fear about something you are going to do or experience.

- Ask students which would probably cause you to have a feeling of trepidation, tossing a ball up in the air or going in front of the whole school to give a speech. Why?
- Have students use facial expressions and body language to show trepidation.

refuge

In the story, the old man hopes that his goats will find refuge during the storm. A refuge is a place you can go to be safe from something.

- Ask what might serve as a refuge during a thunderstorm, an open field or a basement. Explain your answer.
- Have students name reasons that they might need to take refuge somewhere.

grapple

As the storm draws near and the wind picks up speed, the old man grapples with the door to the cave. If you grapple with something or someone, you struggle to hold onto or control them.

- Ask students who they might grapple with, a friend they are wrestling or a teacher who is reading something to them. Why do you think so?
- Have students pretend to grapple with a wild horse they are riding.

Vocabulary in Action

Words About the Story

ridicule

In the story, the villagers make fun of the old man and his goats. You could say that they ridicule him. To ridicule someone or something means to make fun of them.

- Ask students what you might ridicule, a bucket of water or a silly hat you are forced to wear. Explain.
- Have students take turns ridiculing a TV show they saw.

tempest

The old man tells the mayor that a huge storm is coming. Another way to say that is that he tells the mayor that a tempest is about to hit the village. A tempest is a very wild and dangerous storm.

- Ask which is an example of a tempest, a sunny day or a hurricane. Why?
- Have students talk about a tempest that they heard about or were in.

countermand

In the story, the villagers go against the mayor's orders and ring the warning bell. In other words, they countermand his orders. If you countermand an instruction, you cancel it, usually by giving a new instruction.

- Ask students who might be more likely to countermand a mother's instructions, her bratty son or her sweet daughter. Explain your answer.
- Have students countermand some instructions that you give them.

luminous

After the storm passes, the sun shines over the village. Another way to say that is that the sun is luminous. Something that is luminous is bright and seems to shine or give off light.

- Ask which is luminous, a clump of dirt or a streetlight. Why do you think so?
- Have students give examples of things they have seen that are luminous.

THE WALRUS AND THE CARPENTER

In this whimsical poem, a walrus and a carpenter walk along the beach conversing and then trick a bunch of oysters into volunteering to be dinner!

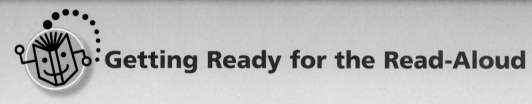

Vocabulary

Words From the Poem

These words appear in blue in the poem. Explain these words after the poem is read.

weep   convenient

beseech   sympathize

Words About the Poem

Explain these words after the poem is read, using context from the poem.

hoax   just

respite   prodigious

Getting Ready for the Read-Aloud

Show students the picture of the walrus and the carpenter on page 76 and read the title aloud. Notice the oyster shells around them. Ask students where they think this poem takes place.

Explain that this narrative poem is from the book *Through the Looking-Glass.* Ask students if they are familiar with this book. Tell students that this classic book is about a girl who travels through a mirror and into a different land. The land on the other side of the mirror is filled with some very unusual characters.

Some phrases in the poem may be new to students. You can briefly explain these as you come to them: *the billows,* the ocean waves; *briny,* salty; *their coats were brushed,* dirt and lint had been removed from their coats; *sealing-wax,* an old way of sealing a letter.

GENRE
Narrative Poem

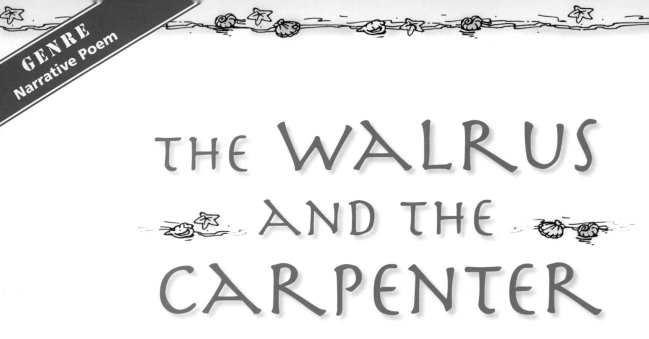

THE WALRUS AND THE CARPENTER

from *Through the Looking-Glass*

By Lewis Carroll
Illustrated by John Tenniel

The sun was shining on the sea,
Shining with all his might:
He did his very best to make
The billows smooth and bright—
And this was odd, because it was
The middle of the night.

The moon was shining sulkily,
Because she thought the sun
Had got no business to be there
After the day was done—
"It's very rude of him," she said,
"To come and spoil the fun!"

The sea was wet as wet could be,
The sands were dry as dry.
You could not see a cloud, because
No cloud was in the sky:
No birds were flying overhead—
There were no birds to fly.

The Walrus and the Carpenter
Were walking close at hand;
They **wept** like anything to see
Such quantities of sand:
"If this were only cleared away,"
They said, "it would be grand!"

Bringing the Poem to Life

Infuse your voice with humor while still being matter-of-fact about the various impossible things that take place. Use different voices for the different characters. Act out some parts, such as the elder oyster shaking his head and the walrus crying melodramatically. Play with the repetitions of "And this was odd."

Why is the moon upset with the sun?

Can you imagine clearing away all the sand on a beach? What do you think would be left?

"If seven maids with seven mops
Swept it for half a year,
Do you suppose," the Walrus said,
"That they could get it clear?"
"I doubt it," said the Carpenter,
And shed a bitter tear.

"O Oysters, come and walk with us!"
The Walrus did **beseech**.
"A pleasant walk, a pleasant talk,
Along the briny beach:
We cannot do with more than four,
To give a hand to each."

The eldest Oyster looked at him,
But never a word he said:
The eldest Oyster winked his eye,
And shook his heavy head—
Meaning to say he did not choose
To leave the oyster-bed.

> Why do you think the eldest Oyster didn't want to join the Walrus and the Carpenter?

But four young Oysters hurried up,
All eager for the treat:
Their coats were brushed, their faces washed,
Their shoes were clean and neat—
And this was odd, because, you know,
They hadn't any feet.

Four other Oysters followed them,
And yet another four;
And thick and fast they came at last,
And more, and more, and more—
All hopping through the frothy waves,
And scrambling to the shore.

The Walrus and the Carpenter
Walked on a mile or so,
And then they rested on a rock
Conveniently low:
And all the little Oysters stood
And waited in a row.

"The time has come," the Walrus said,
"To talk of many things:
Of shoes—and ships—and sealing-wax—
Of cabbages—and kings—
And why the sea is boiling hot—
And whether pigs have wings."

"But wait a bit," the Oysters cried,
"Before we have our chat;
For some of us are out of breath,
And all of us are fat!"
"No hurry!" said the Carpenter.
They thanked him much for that.

"A loaf of bread," the Walrus said,
"Is what we chiefly need:
Pepper and vinegar besides
Are very good indeed—
Now if you're ready, Oysters dear,
We can begin to feed."

> What do you think is for dinner?

"But not on us!" the Oysters cried,
Turning a little blue.
"After such kindness, that would be
A dismal thing to do!"
"The night is fine," the Walrus said.
"Do you admire the view?

"It was so kind of you to come!
And you are very nice!"
The Carpenter said nothing but
"Cut us another slice:
I wish you were not quite so deaf—
I've had to ask you twice!"

"It seems a shame," the Walrus said,
"To play them such a trick,
After we've brought them out so far,
And made them trot so quick!"
The Carpenter said nothing but
"The butter's spread too thick!"

"I weep for you," the Walrus said:
"I deeply **sympathize**."
With sobs and tears he sorted out
Those of the largest size,
Holding his pocket-handkerchief
Before his streaming eyes.

"O Oysters," said the Carpenter,
"You've had a pleasant run!
Shall we be trotting home again?"
But answer came there none—
And this was scarcely odd, because
They'd eaten every one.

Talking About the Poem

Ask students what happened to the Oysters.

Ask students to describe what they liked or did not like about the Walrus, the Carpenter, and the Oysters.

Words From the Poem

weep

In the poem, the Walrus and the Carpenter wept when they saw the large amounts of sand on the beach. If you weep, you cry about a great sadness.

- Ask students which might cause them to weep, if a friend died or if a friend came to visit. Why do you think so?
- Have students pretend to weep.

beseech

In the poem, the Walrus and the Carpenter beseech the Oysters to come walk with them. If you beseech someone, you beg them in an anxious way.

- Ask who might be beseeching someone, a boy asking his parents if they can eat out at a restaurant rather than have meatloaf surprise again or the parents telling the boy that they'll be getting dinner at a restaurant. Explain your answer.
- Ask students to take turns beseeching each other to take a walk with them.

convenient

In the poem, the Walrus and the Carpenter stop to rest on a conveniently low rock. Something that is convenient is handy because it is easy to use or works well in a particular situation.

- Ask students which would be more convenient, a ladder when they are trying to reach something high off the ground or a fork when they are trying to eat soup. Explain.
- Have students give examples of items that would be convenient to have if they were going swimming.

sympathize

The Walrus says that he sympathizes with the Oysters after he has eaten them. If you sympathize with someone, you show that you understand their feelings about something.

- Ask students which they would be more likely to sympathize with, a dog that has lost its way or a tree that has lost its leaves. Why is that?
- Ask students to take turns showing sympathy for a poodle having its hair shaved and shaped into big poofs.

Words About the Poem

hoax

The Walrus and the Carpenter play a trick on the Oysters when they invite them for a walk but really eat them for dinner. You could also say that their invitation is a hoax. A hoax occurs when someone creates a pretend situation and tries to make people believe it is real.

- Ask which is a hoax, taking a picture of a frisbee and telling people it is a UFO or taking a picture of a cow and telling people that it is indeed a cow. Explain your answer.

- Have students talk about a time when a hoax was played on them or they played a hoax on someone else.

respite

After walking so far, the Oysters asked for a moment to catch their breath. You could also say that the Oysters asked for a respite. If you get a respite from something you don't like, you get a short break from it.

- Ask students when they might want a respite, while taking a nap or while doing chores. Why is that?

- Ask students to give examples of things they might want a respite from.

just

In the poem, the Walrus and the Carpenter are not fair to the Oysters. You could also say they are not just. If something is just, it is fair and right.

- Ask students which is more just, waiting for their turn in line or skipping to the head of a line. Explain.

- Have students talk about a time when they were treated in a just way.

prodigious

In the poem, the moon is upset that the sun is out at night because the sun is so much more impressive than the moon. You could also say that the sun is more prodigious than the moon. Something that is prodigious is very large and impressive.

- Ask when a tree might seem prodigious, when it is a full-grown oak tree or when it is still a nut.

- Have students name some things that are prodigious.

Summer Plans

In this story, a girl named Faye finds her plans ruined when her family goes to Alabama for the summer. She soon finds, however, that sometimes life is better when things don't turn out the way you planned them.

Vocabulary

Words From the Story

These words appear in blue in the story. Explain these words after the story is read.

gritty   vie

ailment   jostle

spur

Words About the Story

Explain these words after the story is read, using context from the story.

traverse   precarious

mediocre

Getting Ready for the Read-Aloud

Show students the picture of Faye and her sisters on page 84 and read the title aloud. Explain that they are sitting on the beach and waiting for a special ocean event that may or may not happen. Ask students if they think the sisters are excited about this event.

Explain that this story is about a girl whose family travels far from home for an entire summer. This doesn't fit into Faye's plan, so she pretends to be sick, thinking that her parents will let her stay home if she has a disease.

There are some words and phrases in the story that may be new to students. You might wish to briefly explain these words and phrases as you come to them: *Mandarin*, a Chinese language; *malaria*, a disease that occurs in tropical areas; *yellow fever*, another disease that occurs in tropical areas; *dogsled racing*, a sport in which teams of 3–24 dogs pull people on sleds over snow.

Summer Plans

By Carla Shiflet

Illustrated
by Elizabeth Sayles

The summer before Faye went into sixth grade, her parents rented out a tiny beach cottage in Mobile, Alabama. She had heard them discuss the plans months in advance, their hushed voices drifting down the hall and under her door at night after they thought she and her sisters were asleep. Her father had been offered a job at the University of South Alabama teaching Mandarin for a summer language program. She heard her parents, who sounded very pleased with themselves for having the idea, discuss renting a house on Mobile Bay so that their daughters could have an exciting summer vacation. As soon as Faye grasped what was going on—a whole summer away from her friends, stranded on a hot, sticky, **gritty** beach—she put a plan into effect, calling it "Operation: Exotic Disease."

Bringing the Story to Life

This story is about Faye's self-discovery. Read the early paragraphs in the tone of someone who is irritated. Once the family is vacationing in Alabama, use a disdainful tone of voice. Later, read with an intrigued tone as Faye becomes interested in the jubilee.

Is Faye excited about spending the summer on Mobile Bay?

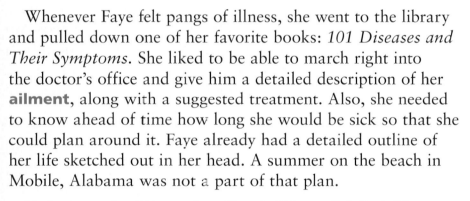

Whenever Faye felt pangs of illness, she went to the library and pulled down one of her favorite books: *101 Diseases and Their Symptoms*. She liked to be able to march right into the doctor's office and give him a detailed description of her **ailment**, along with a suggested treatment. Also, she needed to know ahead of time how long she would be sick so that she could plan around it. Faye already had a detailed outline of her life sketched out in her head. A summer on the beach in Mobile, Alabama was not a part of that plan.

Unfortunately, "Operation: Exotic Disease" failed. Her mother didn't believe for a second that she had malaria. Her father only laughed at her when she attempted yellow fever and told her that the yellow highlighter she had used to color her face was bleeding onto her shirt. It didn't help that both of her sisters seemed completely unbothered by the trip. Her older sister Li (old enough to barely even talk to Faye anymore) was looking forward to working on her tan. They used to be friends, but now Li only wanted to talk on the phone, drink diet sodas, and lock herself in the bathroom. Corinna wasn't on her side either. The summer before, her younger sister (young enough to sometimes pick her nose in public) went to a special day camp where she learned about ocean life.

At the end of the camp, they presented her with a certificate reading: "Corinna Wong, Junior Marine Biologist." When Corinna found out about the beach cottage, she would not stop jabbering on and on about how she, as a junior marine biologist, would need to spend long hours on the beach. Faye felt outnumbered. She tried to win her little sister over by describing shark attacks and jellyfish stings, but Corinna would only look at her blankly and repeat, "I love it. I'm a junior marine biologist."

So at the end of May, Faye found herself making the long trip across the country from Oregon to Alabama, crammed into a sticky station wagon with her parents, her sisters, and their dog, Mr. Sniff. And then she found herself in a tiny, equally sticky beach house with nothing to do all day. The house squatted on tall poles almost right at the edge of the ocean, which excited everyone but Faye. She thought the house looked a little wobbly, like it might fall over or blow away. Her mother sat under a huge, red beach umbrella and watched Corinna splash in the surf or poke at poor ocean creatures that had the misfortune to be crawling by. Li sprawled all day in the sun wearing huge, black sunglasses, twisting her arms and legs into strange positions to make sure the sun shone on every surface of her skin. Faye didn't like the heat and chose to stay within the cool walls of the cottage. She snuck spoonfuls of leftover mango pudding from the refrigerator and read the library books she had brought along.

> If you were at this cottage, would you feel more like Corinna, Li, or Faye?

Most of the books were about dogsled racing. Johnny Hernandez had given a report on it in social studies class the month before, and Faye decided to become a professional dogsled racer. She had a lot of planning to do with such a late start. Her first plan, to be a baker, fell through after her fifth batch of ruined sugar cookies. But a dogsled racer—that was something she could definitely handle, as long as she managed to convince her parents to move to Alaska. Already, she knew the basic commands, and practiced dog training on Mr. Sniff.

On the third day at the beach, the mango pudding ran out, and Faye had already read each of her books four times. She sat on the couch and stared hard at the wall. Then she squeezed her eyes shut to help her concentrate, but she still couldn't imagine herself in Alaska. She put her arms out in front of her, pretending to **spur** on a pack of dogs, but the sound of the ocean kept chasing away her daydreams of ice and snow. Mr. Sniff jumped onto the couch beside her, and she pulled the small dog into her lap.

"Haw," Faye whispered into his ear, turning his body to the left. "Haw." He tried to squirm out of her hands. "Mr. Sniff, you have to practice if we're going to **vie** for the big race trophies," Faye said.

"'Haw' means turn left, and 'gee' means turn right," she explained patiently, although Mr. Sniff had heard the speech many times before.

The back door slid open, and her sisters and mother came in, their faces flushed from the sun.

"Please, please, please," Corinna chanted.

Li rolled her eyes and pushed past them to go into the bathroom. The lock clicked behind her. In all of the commotion, Mr. Sniff had managed to squirm out of Faye's hands and scamper to the back of the house, out of her reach.

"Mush!" Faye called after him, hoping that hearing the sled dog command that means "go dogs, run fast" while he was actually running fast would help him remember.

She went into the kitchen, where Corinna tugged on her mother's arm.

"I don't know, I don't like the idea of you spending the night on the beach by yourself," Faye's mother said, working her wrist out of Corinna's grasp.

Corinna paused for a moment and then exclaimed, "Li will stay with me!"

"No I won't!" Li called from the bathroom.

"What's going on?" Faye asked.

"Someone told Corinna that there might be a jubilee tonight," Faye's mother explained.

"Um, OK," Faye said. "Am I supposed to know what that means?"

> Spending the night on the beach by herself? Why do you think Corinna wants to do that?

Corinna loved any excuse to talk, and when she talked about something that excited her, she talked faster and faster, not stopping for breath, and her voice got higher and higher.

"A jubilee only happens every once in a while, almost never, and no one even knows when, and it's when everything in the ocean decides to come to land, and they all swim up at the same time, and you get to see all of them, and there are crabs, and, um, blue crabs, and horseshoe crabs, and shrimp, and fish!"

"Mom, I don't think that really happens," Faye said. "It doesn't even make sense."

"Well, actually it does; I've heard about it before. Sometimes the amount of air in the ocean drops suddenly, and the fish get confused. They swim to land trying to find somewhere to breathe," Faye's mother said. "It's a very exciting event for people here, because they can easily catch a lot of fish. Then they don't have to worry about buying food for a long time."

"And it's cool!" Corinna shrieked.

"Weird," Faye said. She left the kitchen to look for Mr. Sniff. He had a lot more practicing to do. For a couple of seconds, she felt a twinge of regret that she hadn't decided to be a marine biologist like Corinna. The whole jubilee thing sounded really cool. But she had put too much planning into dogsled racing to change careers now. Besides, she couldn't copy her little sister!

Do you think the jubilee sounds cool?

Even so, she couldn't help but be excited later that night as she helped Li spread out blankets over the sand.

"Look, you twerps," Li said. "I'm only doing this because Mom promised to buy me a new bathing suit if I stayed with you. Don't think for a second that I'm doing this out of the goodness of my heart."

Corinna **jostled** Faye, trying to get her attention. Faye tried to copy Li's blank, bored expression. They all sat down on the blanket and pulled another blanket over their legs. Li switched on a flashlight and started thumbing through a fashion magazine.

"I just know it will happen," Corinna whispered. "It's going to be so great."

Faye stretched back on the blanket with her arms under her head. She closed her eyes and felt the damp, salty wind blow over her face. At first, she tried to pretend that the wind was cold and icy, and that she was standing on a sled, but she stopped. She liked knowing it was beach wind and that she was lying between her two sisters. The moon shone above them like a perfect thumbnail in the sky. Faye pretended not to see when her parents slipped out of the cottage and quietly spread a blanket a few yards behind her and her sisters. She thought Li would get up and go inside if she thought she didn't have to stay to watch Corinna. She stiffened when she saw Li turn and notice their parents, but Li only turned back around and tossed her hair. And as the night unfolded, she even started to talk to Faye and Corinna. They whispered back and forth for what seemed like hours, until Corinna, and then Li, and then finally Faye, fell asleep.

> They're all falling asleep. Do you think they are going to miss the jubilee?

Hours later, they woke to chaos. Lanterns dotted the beach, shedding a flood of light into the otherwise pitch-black night. People swarmed over the sand. They dragged buckets and round, tin wash tubs like the kind in Faye's backyard that she used to wash Mr. Sniff. One couple hurried by pulling a blue plastic wading pool between them. Faye blinked away sleep and squinted toward the ocean.

Slowly, she realized that the beach had transformed into a blanket of squirming, slippery creatures. Fish flopped out of the waves onto the beach and the ones still in the ocean swam in slow, rhythmic motions. Crabs scuttled one way, and then the other. A few feet away, Faye saw an eel that had buried its tail in the wet sand. Its head squirmed in the air, as though searching for something. It was as if the ocean had emptied its blue pockets onto the beach. All of the creatures seemed to be in a slow, stunned state of panic.

> So the jubilee *is* real!

Beside her, Corinna began to sniffle.

"They can't breathe," she said quietly. "And no one is helping them; they're just trying to catch them."

Li snorted. "Yeah, Corinna, what did you think this would be like? Of course people are catching them; it's free food."

Corinna began to cry, and Li's face softened. She pulled Corinna into her lap.

"Shhh, it's OK. It's OK," Li murmured into Corinna's hair, rocking her back and forth.

"Are they going to die?" Corinna asked, gulping for air between sobs.

A tall, gray-haired man passing by heard her question. He paused, resting a laundry basket half full of shrimp on his hip.

"Don't worry, honey," he drawled, "the ones that aren't caught are usually alright. The tide carries them back into the ocean."

Faye stood and walked across the sand at the edge of the water. She knelt to look at a blue crab that crawled sluggishly across the sand, waving its pinchers. She liked the idea of training animals, of teaching a dog to run fast when it hears "mush," but she also liked this random act of nature.

"This is nice," she thought. "Not knowing if something like this would happen, and then having it happen."

She felt strange, admitting that she liked something that happened without her carefully plotting it out. She pushed her fists into the pockets of her jacket and jogged back across the beach to her sisters.

Talking About the Story

Have students summarize how Faye's attitude changed throughout the story. Ask them why they think it changed.

Ask students to talk about a time when they did something they did not want to do and ended up liking it.

Vocabulary in Action

Words From the Story

gritty

In the story, Faye imagines that the beach will be gritty. Something that is gritty has very small pieces of stone in or on it, or feels like it does.

- Ask students which is gritty, sandpaper or a window. Explain.
- Have students describe something they think is gritty.

ailment

Whenever Faye feels sick, she likes to look through her book of diseases so she can describe her ailment to the doctor. When you have an ailment, you are sick, but not too seriously.

- Ask students what is an ailment, a blanket or a cold. Why?
- Have students pretend to have an ailment.

spur

In the story, Faye pretends to spur on a pack of dogs. If something spurs you on, it encourages you to start doing something or to do something faster.

- Ask which is an example of something that would spur you to do your homework faster, knowing you'll get to go out and play when you're done or knowing you'll have to do chores when you're done. Explain your answer.
- Have students discuss a time when something spurred them on.

vie

Faye tells Mr. Sniff that they are going to vie for the big dog racing trophies. If you and other people vie for something, you compete with each other to get it.

- Ask students who is vying for something, two actors trying to win the same award or two actors going to lunch. Why do you think so?
- Have students use competitive facial expressions to pretend they are vying for something.

jostle

In the story, Corinna jostles Faye to get her attention. If something or someone jostles you, they bump or push you in an annoying way.

- Ask what is an example of someone jostling you, someone hugging you or someone elbowing you. Explain why.
- Have students use their hands and bodies to pretend that they're jostling someone.

Vocabulary in Action

Words About the Story

traverse

In the story, Faye and her family travel across the country from Oregon to Alabama. You could say that they traverse the country. If you traverse something, you travel over or across it.

- Ask who is traversing something, a boy walking across a room or a girl sitting on a table. Why?
- Have students use the fingers on one hand to traverse the length of their other arm.

mediocre

Faye's first few days in Alabama are nothing special, but they aren't bad, either. Another way to say that is that her first few days are mediocre. Something that is mediocre is just okay. It's not the worst, but it's not the best either.

- Ask students which is mediocre, getting to play video games as often as you want or getting to play video games once a week. Explain your answer.
- Have students share some things that happened today that were mediocre.

precarious

Faye thinks the beach cottage looks like it might fall off of its tall poles at any second. In other words, Faye thinks the cottage sits precariously on its poles. A thing or situation that is precarious is shaky and unsure. It might break down or change at any time.

- Ask what is precarious, a glass of lemonade on the edge of a table or a bucket full of lemons. Why do you think so?
- Have students place their pencils or pens precariously on the edge of their desks.

THE DUKE

This biography relates the musical career, from a kid who disliked the piano to a master maestro loved by millions, of one of jazz's finest artists, Duke Ellington.

Vocabulary

Words From the Story

These words appear in blue in the story. Explain these words after the story is read.

notion	swanky
flair	improvise
exclusive	

Words About the Story

Explain these words after the story is read, using context from the story.

forte	lucrative
melodious	

Getting Ready for the Read-Aloud

Show students the picture of Duke Ellington on page 94. Have them notice the colors and musical notes swirling out of the piano.

Explain that this article is about a famous ragtime and jazz musician. Ask students to share what they know about ragtime and jazz music. Explain that these types of music generally feature a piano, trumpet, saxophone, drums, and cymbals. Explain that jazz is an energetic type of music that was developed by southern African-American musicians in the late 1800s and early 1900s.

The following words and phrases occur in the story and can be briefly explained as you come to them: *cats*, jazz players; *swing*, to be exciting and lively; *breezy*, smooth and good; *a soul-rousing romp*, an exciting time; *press on the pearlies*, play the piano; *flashy threads*, eye-catching clothes; *pomade*, a hair product like hair gel or mousse; *honky-tonks*, music clubs; *jambalaya*, a spicy mix of rice and meat (shrimp, oysters, or chicken); *cuttin' the rug*, dancing excitedly; *ivory eighty-eights*, piano keys.

THE DUKE

By Andrea Davis Pinkney
Illustrated by Brian Pinkney

This biography is filled with musical rhythms and poetic vernacular. Capture the jazzy feeling by delivering slang-ridden sentences in an ultra-cool and fun way. Tap your fingers to imitate Duke's piano playing. Slap your chair or the wall to mimic percussion instruments. Use your hands to mimic the playing of the saxophone, trombone, and trumpet.

You ever hear of the jazz-playin' man, the man with the cats who could swing with his band? He was born in 1899, in Washington, D.C. Born Edward Kennedy Ellington. But wherever young Edward went, he said, "Hey, call me Duke."

Duke's name fit him rightly. He was a smooth-talkin', slick-steppin', piano-playin' kid. But his piano playing wasn't always as breezy as his stride. When Duke's mother, Daisy, and his father, J. E., enrolled him in piano lessons, Duke didn't want to go. Baseball was Duke's idea of fun. But his parents had other **notions** for their child.

Duke had to start with the piano basics, his fingers playing the same tired tune—*one-and-two-and-one-and-two*. Daisy and J. E. made Duke practice day after day.

To Duke, *one-and-two* wasn't music. He called it an *umpy-dump* sound that was headed nowhere worth following. He quit his lessons and kissed the piano a fast good-bye.

Do you think this is the last of him playing the piano?

Years later, on a steamy summer night, Duke heard that *umpy-dump* played in a whole new way. Folks called the music ragtime—piano that turned *umpy-dump* into a soul-rousing romp.

The ragtime music set Duke's fingers to wiggling. Soon he was back at the piano, trying to plunk out his own ragtime rhythm. *One-and-two-and-one-and-two* . . . At first, this was the only crude tinkling Duke knew.

But with practice, all Duke's fingers rode the piano keys. Duke started to play his own made-up melodies. Whole notes, chords, sharps, and flats. Left-handed hops and right-handed slides.

Believe it, man. Duke taught himself to press on the pearlies like nobody else could. His *one-and-two-umpy-dump* became a thing of the past. Now, playing the piano was Duke's all-time love.

When Duke was nineteen, he was entertaining ladies and gents at parties, pool halls, country clubs, and cabarets. He had fine-as-pie good looks and flashy threads. He was a ladies' man, with **flair** to spare. And whenever a pretty-skinned beauty leaned on Duke's piano, he played his best music, compositions smoother than a hairdo sleeked with pomade.

It wasn't long before Duke formed his own small band, a group of musicians who played all over Washington, D.C. But soon they split the D.C. scene and made tracks for New York City—for Harlem, the place where jazz music ruled.

They called themselves the Washingtonians, and performed in all kinds of New York City honky-tonks. Barron's **Exclusive**. The Plantation. Ciro's. And the Kentucky Club. Folks got to know the band by name and came to hear them play.

Then, on an autumn day in 1927, Lady Luck smiled pretty on the Washingtonians. They were asked to play at the Cotton Club, Harlem's **swankiest** hangout, a big-time nightspot.

The Cotton Club became a regular gig for Duke and his band. They grew to twelve musicians and changed their name to Duke Ellington and His Orchestra. Night after night, they played their music, which was broadcast live over the radio.

> Wow! A lot of people must want to hear him play!

For all those homebodies out in radio-lovers' land—folks who only dreamed of sitting pretty at the Cotton—the show helped them feel like they were out on the town. Duke's *Creole Love Call* was spicier than a pot of jambalaya. His *Mood Indigo* was a musical stream that swelled over the airwaves.

Sometimes the Orchestra performed their tunes straight-up. But other nights, when the joint started to jump, Duke told his band to play whatever came to mind—to **improvise** their solos. To make the music fly! And they did.

Each instrument raised its own voice. One by one, each cat took the floor and wiped it clean with his own special way of playing. Sonny Greer pounded out the bang of jump-rope feet on the street with his snare drum. A subway beat on his bass drum. A sassy ride on his cymbal. Sonny's percussion was smooth and steady. Sometimes only his drumsticks made the music, cracking out the rattly beat of wood slapping wood.

Along with Sonny, Joe "Tricky Sam" Nanton went to work on his trombone, sliding smooth melodic gold. He stretched the notes to their full tilt, pushing and pulling their tropical lilt. When Tricky Sam was through, he'd nod to Otto "Toby" Hardwick. "Your turn," he'd say. "Take the floor, Daddy-O!"

Toby let loose on his sleek brass sax, curling his notes like a kite tail in the wind. A musical loop-de-loop, with a serious twist.

Last came James "Bubber" Miley, a one-of-a-kind horn player. He could make his trumpet wail like a man whose blues were deeper than the deep blue sea. To stir up the sound of his low-moan horn, Bubber turned out a growl from way down in his throat. His gutbucket tunes put a spell on the room.

Yeah, those solos were kickin'. Hot-buttered bop, with lots of sassy-cool tones. When the band did their thing, the Cotton Club performers danced the Black Bottom, the Fish-Tail, and the Suzy-Q. And while they were cuttin' the rug, Duke slid his honey-colored fingertips across the ivory eighty-eights.

Can't you almost hear the music?

The word on Duke and his band spread, from New York to Macon to Kalamazoo and on to the sunshiny Hollywood Hills. The whole country soon swung to Duke's beat. Once folks got a taste of Duke's soul-sweet music, they hurried to the record stores, asking:

"Yo, you got the Duke?"

"Slide me some King of the Keys, please!"

"Gonna play me that Piano Prince and his band!"

People bought Duke's records—thousands of them.

In 1939, Duke hired Billy Strayhorn, a musician who wrote songs. Billy became Duke's ace, his main man. Duke and Billy worked as a team. Together they composed unforgettable music. Billy's song Take the "A" Train was one of the greatest hits of 1941.

With the tunes that he and Billy wrote, Duke painted colors with his band's sound. He could swirl the butterscotch tones of Tricky Sam's horn with the silver notes of the alto saxophones. And, ooh, those clarinets. Duke could blend their red-hot blips with a purple dash of brass from the trumpet section.

In time, folks said Duke Ellington's *real* instrument wasn't his piano at all—it was his Orchestra. Most people called his music jazz. But Duke called it "the music of my people."

What do you think Duke meant by calling jazz "the music of my people"?

Duke introduced a song called *Black, Brown, and Beige* at New York's Carnegie Hall, a symphony hall so grand that even the seats wore velvet. Few African Americans had played at Carnegie Hall before. Duke and his Orchestra performed on January 23, 1943. Outside, the winter wind was cold and slapping. But inside, Carnegie Hall was sizzling with applause. Duke had become a master maestro.

Because of Duke's genius, his Orchestra now had a musical mix like no other.

Now you've heard of the jazz-playin' man. The man with the cats who could swing with his band.

    King of the Keys.

       Piano Prince.

          Edward Kennedy Ellington.

          The Duke.

Talking About the Story

Ask students why people liked Duke's music. Did this story make them want to listen to Duke's music?

Ask students how the music was described in this story. What do they think is the best way to describe music in words?

Vocabulary in Action

notion

Duke's parents had a notion that he would be a piano player. A notion is an idea or belief about something.

- Ask students what they might have a notion about, how to ride a bicycle or how a spaceship works. Why is that?
- Have students say some notions they have about what they're going to do after school.

flair

The biography said that Duke had a lot of flair. If you have flair, you do things in an interesting and stylish way.

- Ask who has more flair, a person who dances when she walks or a person who just walks. Why?
- Have students name a piece of clothing they have that has flair.

exclusive

In the story, Duke and his band play at an exclusive club. An exclusive place, like a club or a store, is one where only certain people are allowed to go.

- Ask which is exclusive, a country club where you have to be a member to get in or a movie theater. Explain.
- Have students say who they would let in and who they would keep out of their own exclusive club.

swanky

The biography describes the Cotton Club as swanky. If you describe a place as swanky, you mean that it is expensive and stylish.

- Ask students which place is swanky, a nice restaurant where you have to wear a suit or dress, or a fast food restaurant. Why do you think so?
- Have students name a swanky place they've heard about or have been to.

improvise

On some nights, Duke had his band members improvise their solos. If you improvise, you do something without a plan and using whatever you have.

- Ask who is improvising, an explorer who has a route mapped out or an explorer who just sets off to see what happens. Explain your answer.
- Have students tell about a time they had to improvise because they didn't know what they were supposed to do.

Vocabulary in Action

Words About the Story

forte

Some people said that Duke's real instrument wasn't the piano, it was his Orchestra. You could say that working his Orchestra was his forte. Something that is your forte is something you are very good at.

- Ask students which might be the forte of a chef, making a cake or juggling. Why do you think so?
- Have students name their own fortes.

melodious

Duke Ellington and His Orchestra made music that people loved to listen to. You could say their music was melodious. A melodious sound is one that is nice to listen to.

- Ask which is melodious, a truck or a symphony. Explain.
- Have students hum melodious sounds.

lucrative

After Duke and His Orchestra started playing at the Cotton Club, they started making a lot of money. You could say that their music was finally lucrative. Something that is lucrative makes you a lot of money.

- Ask which is lucrative, a cookie sale that makes a few dollars or a cookie sale that makes hundreds of dollars. Explain your answer.
- Have students name some activities they wish were lucrative.

The Cat and the Golden Egg

This is a fanciful story about a clever cat that outsmarts a greedy shopkeeper in order to help his poor owner and the people of the village.

Vocabulary

Words From the Story

These words appear in blue in the story. Explain these words after the story is read.

legacy   clamber

mottled   plummet

retort

Words About the Story

Explain these words after the story is read, using context from the story.

avarice   confidant

moral

Getting Ready for the Read-Aloud

Show students the picture of the man and the cat on page 103 and read the title aloud. Explain to them that the two characters are in a store and that the man sitting on the basket of eggs owns the store. Then have them notice that the cat is cutting slices of ham. Ask students if they think the man looks happy about what the cat is doing.

Explain that this is a story about a clever cat who helps his owner. Then tell students that the cat in this story can talk to people. You may also want to mention that gold is a very valuable metal and

that, in this story, people use gold coins or pieces of gold to pay for things.

The following terms occur in the story. You may explain them briefly as you encounter them: *flue,* part of a chimney that smoke travels through; *the town sweep,* the person who cleans chimneys; *tinker,* someone who fixes metal things; *credit,* a promise to pay for something at a later date; *loitering,* hanging around for no reason; *alley rabbit,* an insulting term for a cat; *sallow,* yellowish; *gullet,* throat; *laughingstock,* someone everyone laughs at.

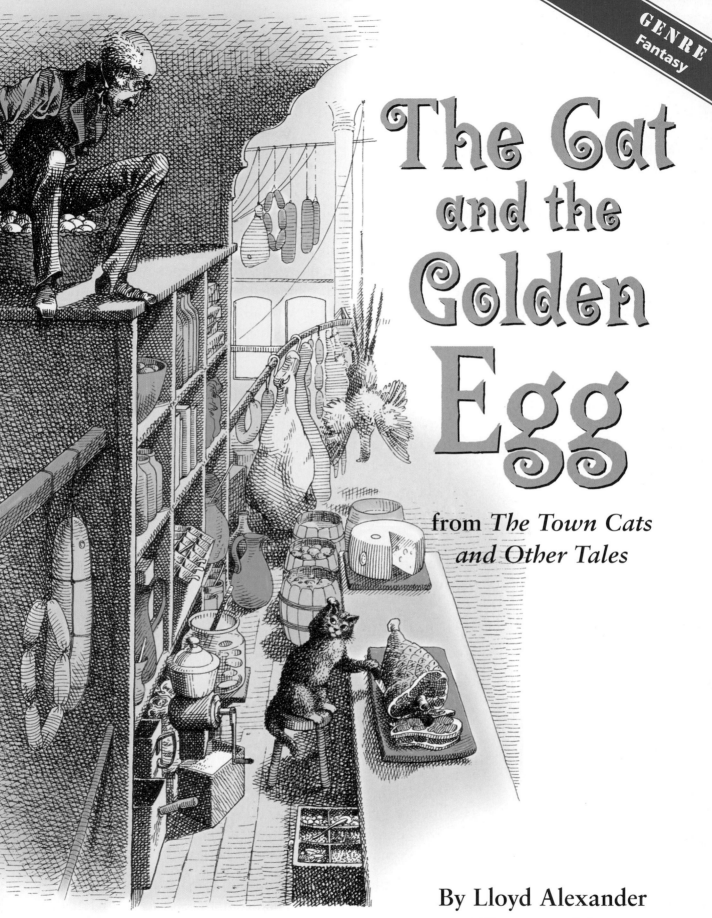

The Cat and the Golden Egg

from *The Town Cats and Other Tales*

By Lloyd Alexander
Illustrated by
Laszlo Kubinyi

Bringing the Story to Life

Read the dialogue with proper inflection for each moment of the story. Be sure to use a soft tone when Dame Agnes is revealing her sadness, a confident tone when Quickset assures her that he has a plan, a facetious tone when Quickset is teasing Grubble in the store, and an indignant tone for Master Grubble. Read the dialogue where Master Grubble clucks like a chicken with exuberance.

Quickset, a silver-gray cat, lived with Dame Agnes, a poor widow. Not only was he a cheerful companion, but clever at helping the old woman make ends meet. If the chimney smoked, he tied a bundle of twigs to his tail, climbed up the flue, and cleaned it with all the skill of the town sweep. He sharpened the old woman's knives and scissors, and mended her pots and pans neatly as any tinker. Did Dame Agnes knit, he held the skein of yarn; did she spin, he turned the spinning wheel.

Now, one morning Dame Agnes woke up with a bone-cracking rheumatism. Her joints creaked, her back ached, and her knees were so stiff she could no way get out of bed.

"My poor Quickset," she moaned, "today you and I must both go hungry."

At first, Quickset thought Dame Agnes meant it was the rheumatism that kept her from cooking breakfast, so he answered:

"Go hungry? No, indeed. You stay comfortable; I'll make us a little broiled sausage and soft boiled egg, and brew a pot of tea for you. Then I'll sit on your lap to warm you, and soon you'll be good as new."

Before Dame Agnes could say another word, he hurried to the pantry. But, opening the cupboard, he saw only bare shelves: not so much as a crust of bread or crumb of cheese; not even a dry bone or bacon rind.

"Mice!" he cried. "Eaten every scrap! They're out of hand, I've been too easy on them. I'll settle accounts with those fellows later. But now, mistress, I had best go to Master Grubble's market and buy what we need."

Dame Agnes thereupon burst into tears. "Oh, Quickset, it isn't mice, it's money. I have no more. Not a penny left for food or fuel."

"Why, mistress, you should have said something about that before now," replied Quickset. "I never would have let you come to such a state. No matter, I'll think of a way to fill your purse again. Meantime, I'll have Master Grubble give us our groceries on credit."

"Grubble? Give credit?" Dame Agnes exclaimed. "You know the only thing he gives is short weight at high prices. Alas for the days when the town had a dozen tradesmen and more: a baker, a butcher, a greengrocer, and all the others. But they're gone, thanks to Master Grubble. One by one, he's gobbled them up. Schemed and swindled them out of their businesses! And now he's got the whole town under his thumb, for it's deal with Grubble or deal with no one."

"In that case," replied Quickset, "deal with him I will. Or, to put it better, he'll deal with me."

The old woman shook her head. "You'll still need money. And you shall have it, though I must do something I hoped I'd never have to do.

"Go to the linen chest," Dame Agnes went on. "At the bottom, under the good pillowslips, there's an old wool stocking. Fetch it out and bring it to me."

Puzzled, Quickset did as she asked. He found the stocking with a piece of string tied around the toe and carried it to Dame Agnes, who undid the knot, reached in and drew out one small gold coin.

"Mistress, that's more than enough," said Quickset. "Why did you fret so? With this, we can buy all we want."

Instead of being cheered by the gold piece in her hand, Dame Agnes only sighed:

"This is the last of the small savings my dear husband left to me. I've kept it all these years, and promised myself never to spend it."

Quickset sounds very determined! What do you think he means by "he'll deal with me"?

"Be glad you did keep it," said Quickset, "for now's the time you need it most."

"I didn't put this by for myself," Dame Agnes replied. "It was for you. I meant to leave it to you in my will. It was to be your **legacy**, a little something until you found another home. But I see I shall have to spend it. Once gone, it's gone, and that's the end of everything."

Why is Dame Agnes so sad about spending the gold coin on the food that she needs?

At this, Dame Agnes began sobbing again. But Quickset reassured her:

"No need for tears. I'll see to this matter. Only let me have that gold piece a little while. I'll strike such a bargain with Master Grubble that we'll fill our pantry with meat and drink a-plenty. Indeed, he'll beg me to keep the money and won't ask a penny, that I promise."

"Master Grubble, I fear, will be more than a match even for you," Dame Agnes replied. Nevertheless, she did as Quickset urged, put the coin in a leather purse, and hung it around his neck.

Quickset hurried through town to the market, where he found Master Grubble sitting on a high stool behind the counter. For all that his shelves were loaded with victuals of every kind, with meats, and vegetables, and fruits, Grubble looked as though he had never sampled his own wares. There was more fat on his bacon than on himself. He was lean-shanked and sharp-eyed, his nose narrow as a knife blade. His mouth was pursed and puckered as if he had been sipping vinegar, and his cheeks as **mottled** as moldy cheese. At sight of Quickset, the storekeeper never so much as climbed down from his stool to wait on his customer, but only made a sour face; and, in a voice equally sour, demanded:

"And what do you want? Half a pound of mouse tails? A sack of catnip? Out! No loitering! I don't cater to the cat trade."

How would you describe Master Grubble using just one word?

Despite this curdled welcome, Quickset bowed and politely explained that Dame Agnes was ailing and he had come shopping in her stead.

"Sick she must be," snorted Master Grubble, "to send a cat marketing, without even a shopping basket. How do you mean to carry off what you buy? Push it along the street with your nose?"

"Why, sir," Quickset answered, "I thought you might send your shop boy around with the parcels. I'm sure you'll do it gladly when you see the handsome order to be filled. Dame Agnes needs a joint of beef, a shoulder of mutton, five pounds of your best sausage, a dozen of the largest eggs—"

"Not so fast," broke in the storekeeper. "Joints and shoulders, is it? Sausage and eggs? Is that what you want? Then I'll tell you what I want: cash on the counter, paid in full. Or you, my fine cat, won't have so much as a wart from one of my pickles."

"You'll be paid," Quickset replied, "and very well paid. But now I see your prices, I'm not sure I brought enough money with me."

"So that's your game!" cried Grubble. "Well, go and get enough. I'll do business with you then, and not before."

"It's a weary walk home and back again," said Quickset. "Allow me a minute or two and I'll have money to spare. And, Master Grubble, if you'd be so kind as to lend me an egg."

"Egg?" **retorted** Grubble. "What's that to do with paying my bill?"

"You'll see," Quickset answered. "I guarantee you'll get all that's owing to you."

Grubble at first refused and again ordered Quickset from the shop. Only when the cat promised to pay double the price of the groceries, as well as an extra fee for the use of the egg, did the storekeeper grudgingly agree.

Taking the egg from Master Grubble, Quickset placed it on the floor, then carefully settled himself on top of it.

"Fool!" cried Grubble. "What are you doing? Get off my egg! This cat's gone mad, and thinks he's a chicken!"

Quickset said nothing, but laid back his ears and waved his tail, warning Grubble to keep silent. After another moment, Quickset got up and brought the egg to the counter:

"There, Master Grubble, that should be enough."

"What?" shouted the storekeeper. "Idiot cat! You mean to pay me with my own egg?"

"With better than that, as you'll see," answered Quickset. While Grubble fumed, Quickset neatly cracked the shell and poured the contents into a bowl. At this, Grubble ranted all the more:

"Alley rabbit! Smash my egg, will you? I'll rub your nose in it!"

Suddenly Master Grubble's voice choked in his gullet. His eyes popped as he stared into the bowl. There, with the broken egg, lay a gold piece.

> Wow! How did the gold piece get into the egg?

Instantly, he snatched it out. "What's this?"

"What does it look like?" returned Quickset.

Grubble squinted at the coin, flung it onto the counter and listened to it ring. He bit it, peered closer, turned it round and round in his fingers, and finally blurted:

"Gold!"

Grubble, in his fit of temper, had never seen Quickset slip the coin from the purse and deftly drop it into the bowl. Awestruck, he gaped at the cat, then lowered his voice to a whisper:

"How did you do that?"

Quickset merely shook his head and shrugged his tail. At last, as the excited storekeeper pressed him for an answer, he winked one eye and calmly replied:

"Now, now, Master Grubble, a cat has trade secrets just as a storekeeper. I don't ask yours, you don't ask mine. If I told you how simple it is, you'd know as much as I do. And if others found out—"

"Tell me!" cried Grubble. "I won't breathe a word to a living soul. My dear cat, listen to me," he hurried on. "You'll have all the victuals you want. For a month! A year! Forever! Here, this very moment, I'll have my boy take a cartload to your mistress. Only teach me to sit on eggs as you did."

> Why does Grubble agree to give Quickset all the food he wants?

"Easily done," said Quickset. "But what about that gold piece?"

"Take it!" cried Grubble, handing the coin to Quickset. "Take it, by all means."

Quickset pretended to think over the bargain, then answered:

"Agreed. But you must do exactly as I tell you."

Grubble nodded and his eyes glittered. "One gold piece from one egg. But what if I used two eggs? Or three, or four, or five?"

"As many as you like," said Quickset. "A basketful, if it suits you."

Without another moment's delay, Grubble called his boy from the storeroom and told him to deliver all that Quickset ordered to the house of Dame Agnes. Then, whimpering with pleasure, he filled his biggest basket with every egg in the store. His nose twitched, his hands trembled, and his usually sallow face turned an eager pink.

"Now," said Quickset, "so you won't be disturbed, take your basket to the top shelf and sit on it there. One thing more, the most important. Until those eggs hatch, don't say a single word. If you have anything to tell me, whatever the reason, you must only cluck like a chicken. Nothing else, mind you. Cackle all you like; speak but once, and the spell is broken."

"What about my customers? Who's to wait on them?" asked Grubble, unwilling to lose business even in exchange for a fortune.

"Never fear," said Quickset. "I'll mind the store."

"What a fine cat you are," purred Grubble. "Noble animal. Intelligent creature."

Grubble's feelings toward Quickset have really changed! Why?

With that, gleefully chuckling and licking his lips, he **clambered** to the top shelf, hauling his heavy burden along with him. There he squatted gingerly over the basket, so cramped that he was obliged to draw his knees under his chin and fold his arms as tightly as he could; until indeed he looked much like a skinny, long-beaked chicken hunched on a nest.

Below, Quickset no sooner had taken his place on the stool than Mistress Libbet, the carpenter's wife, stepped through the door.

"Why, Quickset, what are you doing here?" said she. "Have you gone into trade? And can that be Master Grubble on the shelf? I swear he looks as if he's sitting on a basket of eggs."

Why is Grubble sitting on a basket of eggs?

"Pay him no mind," whispered Quickset. "He fancies himself a hen. An odd notion, but harmless. However, since Master Grubble is busy nesting, I'm tending shop for him. So, Mistress Libbet, how may I serve you?"

"There's so much our little ones need." Mistress Libbet sighed unhappily. "And nothing we can afford to feed them. I was hoping Master Grubble had some scraps or trimmings."

"He has much better," said Quickset, pulling down one of the juiciest hams and slicing away at it with Grubble's carving knife. "Here's a bargain today: only a penny a pound."

Hearing this, Master Grubble was about to protest, but caught himself in the nick of time. Instead, he began furiously clucking and squawking:

"Cut-cut-cut! Aw-cut!"

"What's that you say?" Quickset glanced up at the agitated storekeeper and cupped an ear with his paw. "Cut more? Yes, yes, I understand. The price is still too high? Very well, if you insist: two pounds for a penny."

Too grateful to question such generosity on the part of Grubble, Mistress Libbet flung a penny onto the counter and seized her ham without waiting for Quickset to wrap it. As she hurried from the store, the tailor's wife and the stonecutter's daughter came in; and, a moment later, Dame Gerton, the laundrywoman.

"Welcome, ladies," called Quickset. "Welcome, one and all. Here's fine prime meats, fine fresh vegetables on sale today. At these prices, they won't last long. So, hurry! Step up!"

As the delighted customers pressed eagerly toward the counter, Master Grubble's face changed from sallow to crimson, from crimson to purple. Cackling frantically, he waggled his head and flapped his elbows against his ribs.

Grubble is very upset, so why won't he stop Quickset?

"Cut-aw-cut!" he bawled. "Cut-cut-aw! Cuck-Cuck! Cock-a-doodle-do!"

Once more, Quickset made a great show of listening carefully:

"Did I hear you a-right, Master Grubble? Give all? Free? What a generous soul you are!"

With that, Quickset began hurling meats, cheese, vegetables, and loaves of sugar into the customers' outstretched baskets. Grubble's face now turned from purple to bilious green. He crowed, clucked, brayed, and bleated until he sounded like a barnyard gone mad.

"Give more?" cried Quickset. "I'm doing my best!"

"Cut-aw!" shouted Grubble and away went a chain of sausages. "Ak-ak-cut-aak!" And away went another joint of beef. At last, he could stand no more:

"Stop! Stop!" he roared. "Wretched cat! You'll drive me out of business!"

Beside himself with fury, Master Grubble forgot his cramped quarters and sprang to his feet. His head struck the ceiling and he tumbled back into the basket of eggs. As he struggled to free himself from the flood of shattered yolks, the shelf cracked beneath him and he went **plummeting** headlong into a barrel of flour.

"Robber!" stormed Grubble, crawling out and shaking a fist at Quickset. "Swindler! You promised I'd hatch gold from eggs!"

"What's that?" put in the tailor's wife. "Gold from eggs? Master Grubble, you're as foolish as you're greedy."

"But a fine cackler," added the laundrywoman, flapping her arms. "Let's hear it again, your cut-cut-awk!"

"I warned you not to speak a word," Quickset told the storekeeper, who was egg-soaked at one end and floured at the other. "But you did. And so you broke the spell. Why, look at you, Master Grubble. You nearly turned yourself into a dipped pork chop. Have a care. Someone might fry you."

With that, Quickset went home to breakfast.

As for Master Grubble, when word spread that he had been so roundly tricked, and so easily, he became such a laughing-stock that he left town and was never seen again. At the urging of the townsfolk, Dame Agnes and Quickset took charge of the market, and ran it well and fairly. All agreed that Quickset was the cleverest cat in the world. And, since Quickset had the same opinion, it was surely true.

Vocabulary in Action

Words From the Story

legacy

In the story, Dame Agnes says that the gold coin was to be her legacy to Quickset. A legacy is something special that someone leaves behind or is remembered for after they are gone.

- Ask students what would be a legacy, a statue someone made that still stands today or the napkin you threw out after dinner yesterday. Why do you think so?
- Have students tell what they think their legacy will be.

mottled

Grubble has mottled cheeks. Something that is mottled is covered with patches of different colors that don't make a pattern.

- Ask students which might be mottled, a spotted dog or a fire engine. Explain.
- Have students talk about things they have seen that are mottled.

retort

When Quickset asks to borrow one of Grubble's eggs, Grubble answers Quickset with a retort. To retort means to reply to someone in an angry way.

- Ask students which is a retort, telling someone you could not eat another bite or telling someone you do not want any more of their disgusting food. Explain your answer.
- Have students practice giving a retort.

clamber

Grubble clambers to the top shelf to sit on the basket of eggs. If you clamber somewhere, you climb there using your hands and feet because it is difficult.

- Ask students where they would clamber, up a very steep hill or down a water slide. Explain why.
- Have students use body language and facial expressions to demonstrate how they would clamber up a tall tree.

plummet

In the story, when the shelf cracks, Grubble goes plummeting into a barrel of flour. If something plummets, it falls a long way very quickly.

- Ask which plummets, a muffin that is dropped off a building or someone swimming laps in a pool. Why?
- Have students hold up their pencils and allow them to plummet into their waiting hands.

Words About the Story

avarice

When Quickset says that he can show Grubble how to make gold coins, Grubble is suddenly willing to give him food because he loves gold so much. You could say that Grubble shows his avarice. Someone's avarice is their greed for money and belongings.

- Ask students who shows avarice, a girl who buys as many dolls as she can for herself or a girl who gives her favorite dolls to her sister. Why do you think so?
- Have students tell about a time that they or someone else showed avarice.

moral

In the story, Quickset helps his owner because he is kind and caring. In other words, he is a moral cat. If you call a person or an action moral, you mean that you think they are good and right.

- Ask which is moral, cheating on a test or not cheating on a test. Why?
- Have students give an example of something or someone they think is moral.

confidant

Dame Agnes feels comfortable talking to Quickset about her troubles. Another way to say that is that he is her confidant. If someone is your confidant, you can talk to them about anything, even private things.

- Ask students who is a confidant, your best friend or the stranger next to you on the bus. Explain why.
- Have students take turns telling what they think makes someone a good confidant.

Beetle Blisters

In this funny story, the new girl at school, Lou, wants her science report in front of the class to be a success, but her secret might not make that easy for her.

Vocabulary

Words From the Story

These words appear in blue in the story. Explain these words after the story is read.

smug   **misconception**

hideous   **fester**

burrow

Words About the Story

Explain these words after the story is read, using context from the story.

perturb   **eradicate**

gumption

Getting Ready for the Read-Aloud

Show students the picture of the kids looking at Lou's hand on page 116 and read the title aloud. Then tell them that the girl in the picture has a secret to share with the students at her new school. Have students notice the looks on the kids' faces. Ask them if they can guess what is on Lou's hand.

Explain to students that this is a story about a new girl at school who wants to fit in. Then tell them that the girl must move to a new town and leave her old friends behind. Also, you may want

to mention to them that medicines are made from many different kinds of things, sometimes even things from plants or animals.

The following phrases occur in the story and can be briefly explained as you come to them: *algae*, single-celled plant-like organisms; *zooplankton*, tiny ocean animals; *carcasses*, lifeless bodies; *carnivorous*, something that only eats meat; *red-breasted nuthatch*, a kind of bird; *revolutionary cure*, a new way of treating an illness that is replacing the old ways of treating it.

Beetle Blisters

By Goldman Miller

Illustrated by Nancy Harrison

Last summer I had to get my warts frozen because we were going to move.

"You'll want to look your best when you make new friends," Mom had said.

But I didn't want to make new friends. I liked my old friends, especially Trish, my very *best* friend. Trish and I did everything together. In fact, it was Trish who had given me the warts on my right hand.

"It won't hurt a bit," the nurse at the clinic said. He dabbed a colorless liquid on my warts. It bubbled and hissed. "It's nitrogen," he said, "a gas so cold it boils at room temperature." When he was done, he let me throw the leftover nitrogen on the carpet. I thought it would sink in and make a wet spot, but it sizzled and vanished with a puff.

My warts didn't vanish, though. For three days my hand hurt terribly—I couldn't write, I couldn't paint, and I couldn't sword fight with Trish. After that, they were the same as ever, but we were too busy moving for Mom to notice. By the time she did, school had already started in the town we moved to.

"We'll get them treated again by our new doctor," she said. "Don't worry."

"I will *not* get my warts frozen again," I said. "It really hurt and it didn't do anything at all."

"Don't you want to get rid of them, Lou?" she asked. "They're not very . . . um . . . attractive."

Mom was right; my warts were ugly. They sprouted like little cauliflowers from the back of my right hand. But I didn't care and I didn't care about making new friends, either. I kept the warts hidden.

Why might Lou not want to make new friends?

"Louise, why do you always have your hand in your sleeve?" asked Mary Kay Nolan during science class. She calls me Louise instead of Lou, even though I asked her not to. She is also class president and the smartest kid in fifth grade—or used to be, anyway.

"Maybe she's cold," said Jason. He's the guy who sits behind me. We sometimes play soccer at recess. "What's it to you, anyway?"

"O.K., everyone," said Mr. Smethers, "let's get back to marine organisms, please. Who can name a tiny animal that floats in the ocean somewhere near the bottom of the food chain?"

Mary Kay's hand shot up, and she wiggled eagerly in her seat.

"Mary Kay?"

"Algae," she announced, looking around the classroom **smugly**.

"Good try, but that's not it," said Mr. Smethers. Mary Kay's face fell. "Anyone else?" he asked.

I waited to see if anyone else knew the answer. No one did, so I raised my hand.

"Zooplankton?" I said. We'd studied marine biology at my old school.

"That's right," said Mr. Smethers as he drew some algae and plankton on the board so we could see the difference. Mary Kay made a sour face at me, then looked down at my hand.

"Eee-yew!" she said, pointing. "Louise has warts!" Everyone in the class turned to look at my hand, which had come out of my sleeve when I raised it. I hurriedly drew it back, but it was too late.

"That is SO gross!" Mary Kay said.

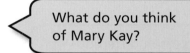

What do you think of Mary Kay?

When I told Mom what had happened, she said, "That's it. You are going to the doctor about those warts, like it or not."

At the clinic, Dr. Lopez told me about a new remedy for warts.

"Extract of the Southern European blister beetle," she said, holding a small vial of amber-colored fluid.

"Beetle juice?" I asked. If Trish had been there, she'd have said Ga-rool! That was a word we used when something was really gross and really cool at the same time. Once she told me about this chamber in the Museum of Natural History where specimen carcasses were picked clean by thousands of carnivorous beetles. That was totally ga-rool.

What is "ga-rool" about a wart?

"Yes, beetle juice." Dr. Lopez chuckled. "And the nice part is, it doesn't hurt much."

"I don't know—," I began, but Mom cut me off.

"Let's do it," she said, giving me the don't-argue eyebrow.

Dr. Lopez rubbed the tops of my warts with a tiny piece of sandpaper until they were rough. Then, using an eyedropper, she squeezed a bead of fluid on top of each wart.

"Expect these to blister a little," she said as she bandaged my hand. "You may want to keep them covered for a while."

The next day, as Mr. Smethers reminded us about our up-coming science reports, Mary Kay leaned over to Brittany Larson and said in a loud whisper, "Louise is trying to hide her **hideous** warts!" They giggled and looked back at me.

"Don't listen to them," said Jason behind me. "They're just stupid."

How is Jason different from Mary Kay?

"Miss Nolan," said Mr. Smethers sternly, "would you like to share something with the class?"

Mary Kay sat up primly and said, "Brittany and I were just discussing my science presentation. It is going to be about birds." Mr. Smethers looked pleased. Everyone knew his hobby was bird-watching.

"Wonderful," he said, "I'm glad you're prepared. Remember, everyone, be ready to give a speech about your topic on Friday."

At recess I thought about my speech on photosynthesis. It wasn't the most interesting subject, but I didn't have any better ideas.

One of my warts began to itch, so I lifted the bandage for a peek.

Whoa! Underneath was the biggest, most disgusting blister I had ever seen: a creamy pus ball the size of a grape surrounded by a fiery red ring, and in the very center sat my wart—greenish and wrinkly—like a rotten raisin on a bun.

> Gross! Have you ever seen a blister like that?

"Ga-rool," I whispered. I rebandaged the blister then checked the others. They had all become totally disgusting. My hand looked like a science experiment.

Science experiment! Why hadn't I thought of it before? My speech could be about warts. They were pretty interesting after all, and when Mary Kay saw I wasn't afraid to talk about them, maybe she would stop teasing me. If I hurried, I could put together a new speech and—

"Want to practice passing?" Jason stood beside me with a soccer ball under his arm. I put my hands behind my back quickly. Had he seen the blisters?

"Sorry, I-I hurt my foot," I said, limping a little for effect. I didn't like to lie, but I didn't want him to see my hands. I mean, a science report about warts was one thing, but showing my disgusting blisters was another.

> Why do you think Lou was afraid that Jason had seen her warts?

"Oh," he said. He looked disappointed. I was glad when the bell rang before he could ask me anything else. I limped inside.

On Friday my blisters were even more gruesome. The outer red rings had deepened to a bruisey shade of purple, and the pus had yellowed noticeably. I brought extra bandages to cover them, because by lunch the sticky stuff had usually worn off the ones I put on in the morning.

Members of the class presented their reports, and I had to admit, Mary Kay's imitation of a redbreasted nuthatch's mating call *was* pretty good. She performed it several times to make sure everyone had a chance to admire her. Mr. Smethers thought it was splendid.

"Well done, Mary Kay," he said. "After lunch, we'll hear from Holly Carter, Jason Maxwell, and Lou Sanchez."

I took the morning's bandages off my blisters, washed my hands, and wrapped the warty one in a paper towel. But when I got back to the classroom, I had an unpleasant surprise: the new bandages were not in my desk! I shuffled through my papers, books, and pencils looking for them, but it was no use. I shut my desk. What could have happened to them?

Where do you think the bandages have gone?

I looked up and saw Mary Kay grinning at me.

"Lose something?" she said.

I was so nervous about standing in front of the class with big, pus-filled blisters that I hardly listened to Holly Carter's report. It was on photosynthesis. I peeked down at my hand. Fluid was oozing out of the wart on my third knuckle. When Holly was finished, I had to clap by slapping one hand against my thigh.

Jason's report was on parasites. He told us about this long worm that can **burrow** right underneath a person's skin, and it has to be pulled out very carefully because if it breaks, it sends a poison into the victim's blood, and death occurs. Boy, I thought, Trish would love that. Jason's pictures of elephantiasis were so amazing, I almost forgot about my blisters.

Almost.

"Your turn, Miss Sanchez," said Mr. Smethers, gesturing toward the front of the room. I awkwardly gathered my materials with my left hand while keeping the paper towel wrapped around my right. People giggled as I tried to put my poster on the easel one-handed. It took me a few tries.

Why does Lou use only one hand to put up her poster?

"My presentation," I said, clearing my throat, "is about warts." The giggles became full-blown laughter. Mary Kay's was the loudest. Suddenly the whole warts thing didn't seem like such a good idea.

I began.

"Throughout history there have been a lot of **misconceptions** about warts," I said. "In some cultures they were thought to have been caused by witches, and a sure cure was to spin a dead cat over your head at the end of a long rope." I had them mesmerized for a moment. Even Mary Kay paused to consider the spinning cat.

"But warts are actually caused by the human papilloma virus, or HPV." As I talked, the class grew more interested. Nobody even noticed that I kept one hand behind my back. Nobody but Mary Kay, that is.

Why did the class start listening to Lou?

"There are some new and unusual cures for warts," I began. But Mary Kay interrupted.

"Like wrapping them in paper towels?" she asked, holding a piece of notebook paper around her own hand. The class started giggling again. I felt myself turning red; worse, I felt a lump growing in my throat. Why did Mary Kay have to be so mean? What had I ever done to her? I looked out at the class.

Jason wasn't laughing. He was mouthing something that looked like *Show her.* He pointed at his hand.

What was Jason telling Lou to do?

Show her?

"Did the paper-towel cure work, or do you need to borrow my cat?" Mary Kay laughed, slapping her desk with the papered hand.

Show her! Jason mouthed again.

I stepped forward and held my hand just in front of her nose.

The class became quiet.

"Why don't you see for yourself?" I said and whipped off the paper towel.

"EE-YEEWW!" Mary Kay pushed herself away from my **festering** blisters, her face pale. "That's . . . that's—" But she didn't finish. Instead, she clapped her hand over her mouth as if she were going to be sick and rushed out of the room.

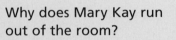

Why does Mary Kay run out of the room?

"*That's,*" I continued smoothly, holding my hand out for everyone to see, "the result of the latest and most revolutionary cure for warts: the powdered wing casings of the Southern European blister beetle, *Cantharis vesicatoria.*"

"Ooooh!" said the class.

"Disgust-o-riffic!" said Jason.

Everyone came forward for a better look, even Mr. Smethers.

The rest of my speech went very well. Better yet, in a few days my blisters—and the warts beneath them—had disappeared completely.

Jason and I play soccer every recess now. I still miss Trish, but I'm not sad all the time anymore. When she visits this summer, the three of us—me, Trish, and Jason—are going to go see the mummy exhibit at the museum.

Oh, and Mary Kay? She's much nicer these days. I wonder if it has anything to do with the large wart on her left thumb?

Talking About the Story

Have students tell why they think Lou decided to do her report on warts. Then ask them what happens when she does.

Ask students to tell about a time when they felt nervous or unsure of themselves but still managed to accomplish something.

Vocabulary in Action

Words From the Story

smug

In the story, Mary Kay is very smug about what she thinks she knows. Someone who is smug is annoyingly happy about how good, smart, or lucky they are.

- Ask students who is smug, someone who gets the last donut and laughs at everyone without one or someone who laughs at a comic strip. Why do you think so?
- Have students practice looking smug.

hideous

Mary Kay describes Lou's warts as being hideous. If something or someone is hideous, they are very ugly and unpleasant.

- Ask students what is hideous, a giant, furry spider or a cute kitten. Explain.
- Have students take turns making hideous faces at one another.

burrow

In Jason's report about parasites, he talks about a long worm that can burrow under people's skin. Something or someone that burrows digs through something or into something.

- Ask who might need to burrow, someone who wants to live in a house in your neighborhood or someone who wants to live underground. Explain your answer.
- Have students tell about some animals that burrow.

misconception

During her report, Lou says that there have been a lot of misconceptions about warts. A misconception is an idea that someone believes but that is not correct.

- Ask which might be a misconception, that drinking water stops the hiccups or that there are 24 hours in a day. Why?
- Have students tell of a misconception that they have had.

fester

In the story, Mary Kay is grossed out when she sees Lou's festering blisters. A festering wound is pus-filled and infected, and the infection is usually spreading.

- Ask what can fester, a poster in your room or a cut on your elbow. Explain why.
- Have students describe something that happened to them that festered.

Vocabulary in Action

Words About the Story

perturb

Lou is upset by Mary Kay's teasing. Another way to say that is that Lou is perturbed by Mary Kay's teasing. Something that perturbs you bothers you a lot.

- Ask when a pet is most likely to perturb you, when jumping on you while you are playing with them or when jumping on you while you are trying to sleep. Explain.
- Have students show how they look when they are perturbed by something.

gumption

In the story, Lou has the courage to speak about her warts in front of her classmates. You could say that she has gumption. If you have the gumption to do something, you have the courage and energy to do it.

- Ask who is showing gumption, a police officer chasing a criminal or a man reading a magazine. Why do you think so?
- Have students give an example of someone they think has gumption.

eradicate

The beetle juice makes all of Lou's warts go away. In other words, the beetle juice eradicates the warts. If you eradicate something, you get rid of it completely.

- Ask which needs to be eradicated, weeds in a lawn or buttons on a shirt. Why?
- Have students tell what things they would like to eradicate.

The Tour

Professional cyclist Lance Armstrong shares his outlook on life and perseverance—and the Tour de France—after surviving cancer.

Vocabulary

Words From the Story

These words appear in blue in the story. Explain these words after the story is read.

oblivion	marvel
parched	prestigious
gallant	smirk

Words About the Story

Explain these words after the story is read, using context from the story.

tribulation	aspire

Getting Ready for the Read-Aloud

Show students the picture of Lance Armstrong on page 129 and read the title aloud. Explain that Armstrong is a cyclist and a cancer survivor. Point out the look of concentration and determination on his face.

Explain that the Tour de France is considered by many to be the greatest bicycle race in the world. The race route loops around most of France. It takes riders on a 2,200-mile ride through open countryside and into the Alps and the Pyrenees mountain ranges. The name of the race literally means "going around France."

The following phrases occur in the story and can be explained briefly as you come to them: *circumference of France,* the perimeter or outside border of France; *an athletic endeavor,* an athletic attempt; *peloton,* a large group of cyclists riding very close together; *psychologically, physically, and emotionally,* mind, body, and heart.

The Tour

from *It's Not About the Bike: My Journey Back to Life*

By Lance Armstrong

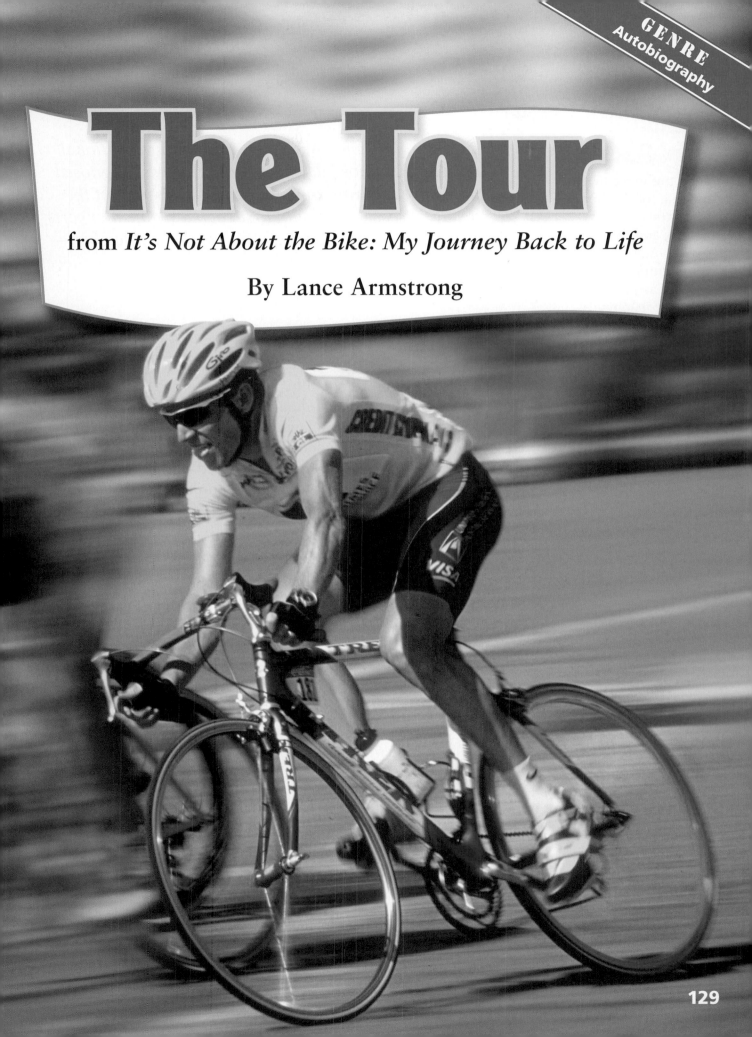

Bringing the Story to Life

24-year-old Lance Armstrong was an international cycling champion, when, in 1996, he was diagnosed with cancer. Armstrong fought to recover from the deadly disease and then pursue what medical experts and skeptics considered an impossible feat for him— winning the Tour de France, a 2,200-mile, three-week bike race.

Life is long—hopefully. But "long" is a relative term: a minute can seem like a month when you're pedaling uphill, which is why there are few things that seem longer than the Tour de France. How long is it? Long as a freeway guardrail stretching into shimmering, flat-topped **oblivion**. Long as fields of **parched** summer hay with no fences in sight. Long as the view of three nations from atop an icy, jagged peak in the Pyrenees.

It would be easy to see the Tour de France as a monumentally inconsequential undertaking: 200 riders cycling the entire circumference of France, mountains included, over three weeks in the heat of the summer. There is no reason to attempt such a feat of idiocy, other than the fact that some people, which is to say some people like me, have a need to search the depths of their stamina for self-definition. (I'm the guy who can take it.) It's a contest in purposeless suffering.

But for reasons of my own, I think it may be the most **gallant** athletic endeavor in the world. To me, of course, it's about living.

A little history: the bicycle was an invention of the industrial revolution, along with the steam engine and the telegraph, and the first Tour was held in 1903, the result of a challenge in the French sporting press issued by the newspaper *L'Auto*. Of the sixty racers who started, only 21 finished, and the event immediately captivated the nation. An estimated 100,000 spectators lined the roads into Paris, and there was cheating right from the start: drinks were spiked, and tacks and broken bottles were thrown onto the road by the leaders to sabotage the riders chasing them. The early riders had to carry their own food and equipment, their bikes had just two gears, and they used their feet as brakes. The first mountain stages were introduced in 1910 (along with brakes), when the peloton rode through the Alps, despite the threat of attacks from wild animals. In 1914, the race began on the same day that the Archduke Ferdinand was shot. Five days after the finish of the race, war swept into the same Alps the riders had climbed.

Today, the race is a **marvel** of technology. The bikes are so light you can lift them overhead with one hand, and the riders are equipped with computers, heart monitors, and even two-way radios. But the essential test of the race has not changed: who can best survive the hardships and find the strength to keep going? After my personal ordeal, I couldn't help feeling it was a race I was suited for.

> Do you think surviving the hardships of cancer helped prepare Armstrong for the hardships of the Tour de France?

Before the '99 season began, I went to Indianapolis for a cancer-awareness dinner, and I stopped by the hospital to see my old cancer friends. Scott Shapiro said, "So, you're returning to stage racing?"

I said yes, and then I asked a question. "Do you think I can win the Tour de France?"

"I not only think you can," he said. "I expect you to."

But I kept crashing.

At first, the 1999 cycling season was a total failure. In the second race of the year, the Tour of Valencia, I crashed off the bike and almost broke my shoulder. I took two weeks off, but no sooner did I get back on than I crashed again: I was on a training ride in the south of France when an elderly woman ran her car off the side of the road and sideswiped me. I suffered like the proverbial dog through Paris-Nice and Milan-San Remo in lousy weather, struggling to mid-pack finishes. I wrote it off to early-season bad form, and went on to the next race—where I crashed again. On the last corner of the first stage, I spun out in the rain. My tires went out from under me in a dusky oil slick and I tumbled off the bike.

I went home. The problem was simply that I was rusty, so for two solid weeks I worked on my technique, until I felt secure in the saddle. When I came back, I stayed upright.

I finally won something, a time-trial stage in the Circuit de la Sarthe. My results picked up.

But it was funny, I wasn't as good in the one-day races anymore. I was no longer the angry and unsettled young rider I had been. My racing was still intense, but it had become subtler in style and technique, not as visibly aggressive. Something different fueled me now—psychologically, physically, and emotionally—and that something was the Tour de France.

What about him had changed?

I was willing to sacrifice the entire season to prepare for the Tour. I staked everything on it. I skipped all the spring classics, the **prestigious** races that comprised the backbone of the international cycling tour, and instead picked and chose only a handful of events that would help me peak in July. Nobody could understand what I was doing. In the past, I'd made my living in the classics. Why wasn't I riding in the races I'd won before? Finally a journalist came up to me and asked if I was entered in any of the spring classics.

"No," I said.

"Well, why not?"

"I'm focusing on the Tour."

He kind of **smirked** at me and said, "Oh, so you're a Tour rider now." Like I was joking.

I just looked at him, and thought, *Whatever, dude. We'll see.*

In 1999, Armstrong put himself through rigorous training geared to the Tour. He practiced key stages, and focused exclusively on this one race. That singular ambition helped Armstrong win the punishing Tour de France that year. It was his first win and one of the most amazing comeback stories in sports history. But that was only the beginning. He went on to win the Tour de France a further six years in a row before retiring in 2005.

Talking About the Story

Have students explain why they think the Tour de France appeals to Armstrong.

Remind students that Armstrong said that "long" is a relative term that depends upon the situation. Ask them to think of occasions when a long time seemed to go by quickly and a short time seemed to take forever.

Vocabulary in Action

Words From the Story

oblivion

Armstrong describes the Tour de France as being as long as a guard rail disappearing into the distant oblivion. Something that is in oblivion is in the situation of being unknown or not remembered.

- Ask students which are lost in oblivion, their memories of being just one year old or their memories from yesterday. Why?
- Have students name some things that have faded into oblivion.

parched

Armstrong describes hay left out in the summer heat as parched. Something that is parched is very, very dry.

- Ask what it feels like to be parched, thirsty or hungry. Why do you think so?
- Have students speak as though their throats are parched.

gallant

Armstrong says that the Tour de France is a gallant athletic event. If you call an action gallant, someone must be brave to try it because it is dangerous and difficult.

- Ask students who is gallant, a firefighter or a coward. Explain your answer.
- Have students name some real or fictional people who they think are gallant. Have them say why they think so.

marvel

The equipment used in modern cycling is a marvel of technology compared to the equipment used 100 years ago. A marvel is something that is wonderful and surprising.

- Ask students which is a marvel, a cup of vanilla ice cream or a foot-tall ice cream sundae with every topping they can imagine. Explain.
- Have students name some things that are marvelous.

prestigious

Armstrong skipped many of the prestigious races so that he could better prepare for the Tour de France. If something is prestigious, people admire and respect it.

- Ask which place is prestigious, a royal palace or a garbage dump. Why is that?
- Have students name some people or places that are prestigious.

smirk

The reporter smirked as if he did not believe that Armstrong was really capable of the Tour de France. If someone smirks, they smile in a mean way because they think they know more than you do.

- Ask students when they might smirk, when teasing a friend or when helping a friend. Why?
- Have students practice smirking at each other.

Words About the Story

tribulation

Riders who enter the Tour de France face all of the difficulties the race produces. You could also say that the riders face the race's tribulations. If a lot of bad things happen to you, you can say you have tribulations.

• Ask students what they might consider a tribulation, having their backpack tear and spill all their books on the floor or getting a new backpack. Why?

• Have students describe the tribulations they have encountered recently.

aspire

Armstrong wanted to win the Tour de France. You could also say that he aspired to win the race. If you aspire to something, you have a special goal that you hope to reach.

• Ask students what they would aspire to, something in the future or something in the past. Explain.

• Have students describe something they aspire to.

CASEY at the BAT

One of America's best-loved poems, *Casey at the Bat*, tells the story of mighty Casey, who has a chance to win an exciting baseball game in front of his Mudville fans.

Vocabulary

Words From the Poem

These words appear in blue in the poem. Explain these words after the poem is read.

patron	**grandeur**
precede	**scornful**
defiance	

Words About the Poem

Explain these words after the poem is read, using context from the poem.

envision	**legendary**
dismal	

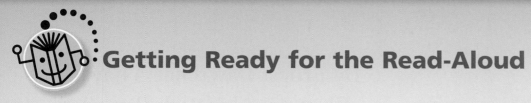

Getting Ready for the Read-Aloud

Show students the picture of Casey on page 136 and read the title aloud. Explain that mighty Casey is at bat waiting for a pitch. Have them notice the determination in his expression and the tension in his stance.

Explain that this poem takes place during the last inning of a baseball game. Ask children to share what they know about baseball. If necessary, explain some basic rules of the game, such as: teams score by hitting the ball and running around the bases to home plate; if a team gets three "outs,"

they lose their chance to score; one way to get an "out" is for a hitter to get three strikes; a hitter gets a strike when he doesn't swing at a ball that is thrown in the strike zone or if he swings at a ball and misses it.

The following phrases occur in the poem and can be briefly explained as you come to them: *died at second,* was tagged out at second base; *a pallor wreathed the features,* the faces were pale; *lightly doffed his hat,* took his cap off for a moment in acknowledgment; *visage,* face.

CASEY at the BAT

By Ernest Lawrence Thayer

Illustrated by Rick Powell

This poem takes place at an exciting baseball game that Mudville is losing two to four. Five thousand Mudville fans watch as their team has one last chance to win the game.

It looked extremely rocky for the Mudville nine that day;
The score stood two to four with but one inning left to play.
So, when Conney died at second, and Burrows did the same,
A pallor wreathed the features of the **patrons** of the game.

A straggling few got up to go, leaving there the rest,
With that hope which springs eternal within the human breast
For they thought: "If only Casey could get a whack at that,"
They'd put even money now, with Casey at the bat.

Some people left before the game was over! Why is that?

But Flynn **preceded** Casey, and likewise so did Blake,
And that former was a pudd'n, and the latter was a fake.
So on that stricken multitude a deathlike silence sat;
For there seemed but little chance of Casey's getting to the bat.

Is it looking good for Mudville?

But Flynn let fly a "single," to the wonderment of all.
And the much-despised Blakey "tore the cover off the ball."
And when the dust had settled, and they saw what had occurred,
There was Blakey safe at second, and Flynn a-hugging third.

Who do you think is up next to bat?

Then from the gladdened multitude went up a joyous yell—
It rumbled in the moutaintops, it rattled in the dell;
It struck upon the hillside and rebounded on the flat—
For Casey, mighty Casey, was advancing to the bat.

There was ease in Casey's manner as he stepped into his place,
There was pride in Casey's bearing and a smile on Casey's face;
And when, responding to the cheers, he lightly doffed his hat,
No stranger in the crowd could doubt 'twas Casey at the bat.

Ten thousand eyes were on him as he rubbed his hands with dirt,
Five thousand tongues applauded as he wiped them on his shirt;
And when the writhing pitcher ground the ball into his hip,
Defiance glanced from Casey's eye, a sneer curled Casey's lip.

And now the leather-covered sphere came hurtling through the air,

And Casey stood a-watching it in haughty **grandeur** there.

Close by the sturdy batsman the ball unheeded sped;

"That ain't my style," said Casey. "Strike one!" the umpire said.

> Wow! Did you think Casey was going to get a strike on the first pitch?

From the benches, black with people, there went up a muffled roar,

Like the beating of the storm waves on a stern and distant shore.

"Kill him! Kill the umpire!" someone shouted from the stand—

And it's likely they'd have killed him had not Casey raised his hand.

With a smile of noble charity great Casey's visage shown;

He stilled the rising tumult. He made the game go on.

He signaled to the pitcher, and once more the spheroid flew;

But Casey still ignored it, and the umpire said, "Strike two!"

"Fraud!" cried the maddened thousands, and the echo answered "Fraud."

But one **scornful** look from Casey and the audience was awed;

They saw his face grow stern and cold, they saw his muscles strain,

And they knew that Casey wouldn't let the ball go by again.

> Casey didn't even try to hit the second ball. It was a good pitch, but the crowd blamed the umpire.

The sneer is gone from Casey's lips, his teeth are clenched in hate,
He pounds with cruel vengence his bat upon the plate;
And now the pitcher holds the ball, and now he lets it go,
And now the air is shattered by the force of Casey's blow.

Oh, somewhere in this favored land the sun is shining bright;
The band is playing somewhere, and somewhere hearts are light;
And somewhere men are laughing, and somewhere children shout;
But there is no joy in Mudville—Mighty Casey has struck out.

What do you think just happened? Let's see.

Talking About the Poem

Have students summarize what happened at the game and tell whether or not they were surprised by the ending.

Ask students if they have ever watched or played a game that was so close, no one knew for sure who would win, even at the very end.

Vocabulary in Action

patron

In the poem, the patrons were the people who had come to watch the baseball game. A patron of something is its regular customer or viewer.

- Ask what might have patrons, a restaurant or a birthday party. Why?
- Have students tell some places or stores they are patrons of.

precede

In the poem, Flynn was one batter who preceded Casey. If something precedes something else, it comes before it.

- Ask what precedes winning a gold medal at the Olympics, a lot of hard work or being real lazy. Why is that?
- Have students form a line and then name the students preceding them in the line.

defiance

Casey's eyes showed his defiance as he waited for the first pitch. Defiance is a way of showing you are not willing to obey someone or something.

- Ask students who is being defiant, the girl who stays up past her bed time or the girl who goes to bed on time. Explain.
- Have students practice displaying body language of defiance.

grandeur

In this poem, Casey is described as having grandeur as he stands at the plate. If something has grandeur, it is impressive because of its size, beauty, or power.

- Ask which building might have grandeur, a royal palace or a backyard treehouse. Why?
- Have students give examples of animals and places that have grandeur.

scornful

Casey gave a scornful look after he struck out the second time. If you are scornful of someone or something, you show no respect for them.

- Ask who is being scornful, the boy who stops to look at a chalk drawing on the sidewalk or the boy who stops to wipe his feet on the chalk drawing. Explain your answer.
- Have students take turns giving a scornful look.

Words About the Poem

envision

The crowd imagined Casey hitting a home run. You might also say they envisioned it. When you envision something, you picture it in your head before it actually happens.

- Ask students what they might envision, what they're planning to be when they grow up or what they did before coming to school. Explain.
- Have students envision what the world will be like in a hundred years and then draw a picture of it.

dismal

It was a bad day for the Mudville fans because Casey struck out. You could also say it was a dismal day. Something that is dismal is depressingly bad.

- Ask students which situation is dismal, finding a dollar under their pillow or finding a fly in their spaghetti. Why?
- Have students describe a day with dismal weather.

legendary

Casey was a well-known player who wowed the fans with his hitting ability. You could also say he was a legendary player. If you describe someone or something as legendary, you mean that they are very famous and that many stories are told about them.

- Ask who might be legendary, a famous singer or someone who only sings in their shower. Why do you say that?
- Have students name examples of legendary people or places, as well as some of the stories that have been told about those people or places.

The Wish

A boy challenges himself with a dangerous journey from his own fantasy, promising himself that his wish will be granted if he just survives till the end.

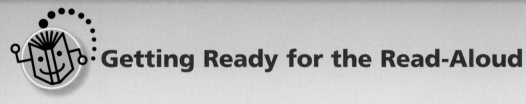

Vocabulary

Words From the Story

These words appear in blue in the story. Explain these words after the story is read.

resist	accurate
vicious	instinctive
clench	

Words About the Story

Explain these words after the story is read, using context from the story.

fanciful	obstruction
jeopardy	

Getting Ready for the Read-Aloud

Show students the picture of the boy and the carpet on pages 144–145. Read the title aloud. Have students notice the intense expression on the boy's face and the swirls of color in the carpet he is walking on. What do they think the colors look like?

Tell students that this story takes place in a very large, very fancy house. Such houses frequently have a grand entranceway, which is a hallway as big as a large room, between the front door and an elaborate staircase. The rug in such an area would have to be very impressive.

The following phrases occur in the story and can be briefly explained as you come to them: *tennis lawn,* a tennis court made of grass; *adder,* a type of snake; *vast tapestry,* large cloth with a rich design; *curiously intent,* unusually focused; *transferring,* moving from one place to another; *properly stuck,* really stuck.

The Wish

By Roald Dahl
Illustrated by Guy Porfirio

Under the palm of one hand the child became aware of the scab of an old cut on his kneecap. He bent forward to examine it closely. A scab was always a fascinating thing; it presented a special challenge he was never able to **resist**.

Yes, he thought, I will pick it off, even if it isn't ready, even if the middle of it sticks, even if it hurts like anything.

Bringing the Story to Life

Begin the story with detached curiosity as the boy looks around for a challenge. As he starts across the carpet, add a tinge of fear to your voice and have it slowly increase. Speak with more intensity when the boy takes steps and more musingly when he pauses to consider his next move. Suddenly revert to a detached narrator's voice for the last sentence to highlight the shock at the end.

With a fingernail he began to explore cautiously around the edges of the scab. He got a nail underneath it, and when he raised it, but ever so slightly, it suddenly came off, the whole hard brown scab came off beautifully, leaving an interesting little circle of smooth red skin.

Nice. Very nice indeed. He rubbed the circle and it didn't hurt. He picked up the scab, put it on his thigh and flipped it with a finger so that it flew away and landed on the edge of the carpet, the enormous red and black and yellow carpet that stretched the whole length of the hall from the stairs on which he sat to the front door in the distance. A tremendous carpet. Bigger than the tennis lawn. Much bigger than that. He regarded it gravely, setting his eyes upon it with mild pleasure. He had never really noticed it before, but now, all of a sudden, the colors seemed to brighten mysteriously and spring out at him in a most dazzling way.

You see, he told himself, I know how it is. The red parts of the carpet are red-hot lumps of coal. What I must do is this: I must walk all the way along it to the front door without touching them. If I touch the red I will be burnt. As a matter of fact, I will be burnt up completely. And the black parts of the carpet . . . yes, the black parts are snakes, poisonous snakes, adders mostly, and cobras, thick like tree trunks round the middle, and if I touch one of *them,* I'll be bitten and I'll die before tea time. And if I get across safely, without being burnt and without being bitten, I will be given a puppy for my birthday tomorrow.

He got to his feet and climbed higher up the stairs to obtain a better view of this vast tapestry of color and death. Was it possible? Was there enough yellow? Yellow was the only color he was allowed to walk on. Could it be done? This was not a journey to be undertaken lightly; the risks were far too great for that. The child's face peered down anxiously over the banisters. The yellow was a bit thin in places and there

What is the wish mentioned in the title?

were one or two widish gaps, but it did seem to go all the way along to the other end. For someone who had only yesterday triumphantly traveled the whole length of the brick path from the stables to the summer-house without touching the cracks, this carpet thing should not be too difficult. Except for the snakes. The mere thought of snakes sent a fine electricity of fear running like pins down the backs of his legs and under the soles of his feet.

Do you think the boy has a good imagination?

He came slowly down the stairs and advanced to the edge of the carpet. He extended one small sandaled foot and placed it cautiously upon a patch of yellow. Then he brought the other foot up, and there was just enough room for him to stand with the two feet together. There! He had started! His bright oval face was curiously intent, a shade whiter perhaps than before, and he was holding his arms out sideways to assist his balance. He took another step, lifting his foot high over a patch of black, aiming carefully with his toe for a narrow channel of yellow on the other side. When he had completed the second step he paused to rest, standing very stiff and still. The narrow channel of yellow ran forward unbroken for at least five yards and he advanced gingerly along it, bit by bit, as though walking a tightrope. Where it finally curled off sideways, he had to take another long stride, this time over a **vicious**-looking mixture of black and red. Halfway across he began to wobble. He waved his arms around wildly, windmill fashion, to keep his balance, and he got across safely and rested again on the other side. He was quite breathless now, and so tense he stood high on his toes all the time, arms out sideways, fists **clenched**. He was on a big safe island of yellow. There was lots of room on it, he couldn't possibly fall off, and he stood there resting, hesitating, waiting, wishing he could stay forever on this big safe yellow island. But the fear of not getting the puppy compelled him to go on.

Can you imagine what the boy looks like as he tries to regain his balance?

Step by step, he edged further ahead, and between each one he paused to decide exactly where he should put his foot. Once, he had a choice of ways, either to left or right, and he chose the left because although it seemed the more difficult, there was not so much black in that direction. The black was what had made him nervous. He glanced quickly over his shoulder to see how far he had come. Nearly halfway. There could be no turning back now. He was in the middle and he couldn't turn back and he couldn't jump off sideways either because it was too far, and when he looked at all the red and all the black that lay ahead of him, he felt that old sudden sickening surge of panic in his chest—like last Easter time, that afternoon when he got lost all alone in the darkest part of Piper's Wood.

He took another step, placing his foot carefully upon the only little piece of yellow within reach, and this time the point of the foot came within a centimeter of some black. It wasn't touching the black, he could see it wasn't touching, he could see the small line of yellow separating the toe of his sandal from the black; but the snake stirred as though sensing his nearness, and raised its head and gazed at the foot with bright beady eyes, watching to see if it was going to touch.

"I'm not touching you! You mustn't bite me! You know I'm not touching you!"

Another snake slid up noiselessly beside the first, raised its head, two heads now, two pairs of eyes staring at the foot, gazing at a little naked place just below the sandal strap where the skin showed through. The child went high up on his toes and stayed there, frozen stiff with terror. It was minutes before he dared to move again.

Do you think the boy is still pretending or is he really in danger?

The next step would have to be a really long one. There was this deep curling river of black that ran clear across the width of the carpet, and he was forced by his position to cross it at its widest part. He thought first of trying to jump it, but decided he couldn't be sure of landing **accurately** on the narrow band of yellow on the other side. He took a deep breath, lifted one foot, and inch by inch he pushed it out in front of him, far far out, then down and down until at last the tip of his sandal was across and resting safely on the edge of the yellow. He leaned forward, transferring his weight to his front foot. Then he tried to bring the back foot up as well. He strained and pulled and jerked his body, but the legs were too wide apart and he couldn't make it. He tried to get back again. He couldn't do that either. He was doing the splits and he was properly stuck. He glanced down and saw this deep curling river of black underneath him. Parts of it were stirring now, and uncoiling and beginning to shine with a dreadfully oily glister. He wobbled, waved his arms frantically to keep his balance, but that seemed to make it worse. He was starting to go over. He was going over to the right, quite slowly he was going over, then faster and faster, and at the last moment, **instinctively** he put out a hand to break the fall and the next thing he saw was this bare hand of his going right into the middle of a great glistening mass of black and he gave one piercing cry as it touched.

Outside in the sunshine, far away behind the house, the mother was looking for her son.

Talking About the Story

Have students summarize the boy's journey across the carpet. Did they think the boy's wish would come true or not?

Ask students if they ever get caught up in their own fantasies.

Vocabulary in Action

Words From the Story

resist

In the story, the boy could not resist picking his scab off his knee. If you resist something, you fight against it and refuse to give in.

- Ask students which boy is resisting coming out from under a table, the one who comes out when told to or the one who has to be dragged out by his ankles while he holds onto the table legs. Why is that?
- Have students talk about when they resisted doing something.

vicious

The boy thought the red and black colors of the carpet looked vicious. If you describe something as vicious, you mean that it is mean and dangerous.

- Ask which animal is more likely to be vicious, a bunny rabbit or a lion. Explain.
- Have students name some people, animals, or fictional characters who are vicious.

clench

The boy clenched his fists as he balanced himself on a safe bit of the rug. When you clench something, you squeeze it tightly.

- Ask which you might clench in your fist, a favorite toy or a wiggling worm. Why do you think so?
- Have students clench their teeth.

accurate

In the story, the boy didn't think he could jump accurately from one yellow bit of carpet to another. If you say something is accurate, you mean that it is exactly correct.

- Ask students which statement is accurate, that they are humans or that they are frogs. Why?
- Have students try to throw a crumpled ball of paper into a trash can and then say if they had accurate aim.

instinctive

At the end of the story, the boy instinctively broke his fall by putting out his hand. A person or animal's action is instinctive if it comes so naturally that they do it without thinking.

- Ask which action is instinctive when crossing hot pavement, running to avoid getting burned or walking slowly. Explain.
- Have students name some other instincts that people or animals have.

Vocabulary in Action

Words About the Story

fanciful

In the story, the boy faces a hard journey he created from his own imagination. You could also say that the journey was fanciful. Something can be called fanciful if it seems like it came from someone's imagination.

- Ask what is more likely to be fanciful, a painting or a photograph. Why?
- Have students develop an idea for a fanciful story.

jeopardy

In his journey across the carpet, the boy was in danger of being burned by lava or bitten by poisonous snakes. You could say that he was in jeopardy. If someone or something is in jeopardy, they are in danger.

- Ask students which person is in jeopardy, the one standing outside in a hail and lightning storm or the one safely inside a house during the storm. Why do you think so?
- Have students think of situations that could place them in jeopardy.

obstruction

The boy is blocked from crossing on yellow carpet by the large swirls of red and black. You could also say that the swirls of red and black were obstructions in the boy's attempt to cross the carpet. Something is an obstruction when it is blocking something else.

- Ask what might be an obstruction to a fun weekend, having a lot of homework or having some beautiful weather. Explain.
- Have students name some things that might be obstructions to learning.

Blindly He Goes ...Up

Erik Weihenmayer's positive attitude and sense of adventure has led him, a blind elementary school teacher, to climb each of the world's highest mountains.

Vocabulary

Words From the Story

These words appear in blue in the story. Explain these words after the story is read.

compel   superb

preempt   embark

endurance

Words About the Story

Explain these words after the story is read, using context from the story.

fervent   intuitive

acclimate

 ## Getting Ready for the Read-Aloud

Show students the picture of Erik Weihenmayer (WINE-mayor) on page 153 and read the title aloud. Explain that Erik is blind, yet he has been able to accomplish amazing feats like climbing Mount Everest, the tallest mountain on Earth!

Ask students what they know about mountain climbing. If necessary, explain that climbers who tackle the world's major peaks must train very hard and face physical challenges such as a lack of oxygen, freezing temperatures, and bad weather.

Explain that mountain climbers often work with guides or in teams to achieve their goals.

As needed, you can briefly explain the following terms in the story: *sherpas,* natives of the Himalayan area who guide mountain climbers; *prosthetic eye,* an artificial eye; *paraglider,* flier on a large kite-like sail; *retina,* the part of the eye that receives images; *Kilimanjaro,* a tall mountain in Africa; *summit,* both the highest point of a mountain and the act of reaching that point; *infinite,* with no end; *guide dog,* a specially trained dog that helps someone with a disability.

Blindly He Goes . . . Up

By Steve Rushin

Bringing the Story to Life

Alternate between reading with humor the various anecdotes of Erik's life and reading with awe about the various achievements Erik has accomplished. Mime some scenes in the story, such as Erik taking out his prosthetic eye or climbing Mount Everest.

How do you think the students felt?

Before he climbed to the summit of Mount Everest four years ago, Erik Weihenmayer (WINE-mayor) felt **compelled** to prove to his disbelieving sherpas that he really was blind. So he pulled down his lower left eyelid, leaned forward and let his prosthetic eye drop into his cupped hand. When he offered to remove his false right eye, the head sherpa, Kami Tenzing, protested **preemptively**, "No, no, no! I believe you!"

But then Weihenmayer's whole life defies belief. As a fifth-grade teacher in Phoenix he once snatched, from the hand of a girl, the crinkling note she was about to pass. Then he threatened to read it to the hushed class. "The kids knew I was blind," he says. "But I was also their teacher, so they figured somehow I'd be able to read it."

While he can't do that, the 36-year-old Weihenmayer is a skydiver, a paraglider and a marathon runner. He has climbed the Seven Summits (the highest peaks on each continent) and completed Primal Quest, billed as the world's most dangerous **endurance** race. After climbing Mount Elbrus, the tallest peak in Europe, Weihenmayer skied the 10,000 feet to base camp. He has scaled the rock face of Yosemite's El Capitan, the icefall of Polar Circus in the Canadian Rockies and—upon returning from Everest—the fiberglass Matterhorn at Disneyland.

Weihenmayer was born legally blind. He suffered from a disease that caused his retinas to slowly split from the inside out, like a wet piece of plywood. By age 13 he was entirely blind. Nevertheless, he became a **superb** high school wrestler. As a teenager he went on exotic hikes with his father, Ed, a Marine pilot in Vietnam. "We were walking from valley to valley on Kilimanjaro, and Erik suddenly says, 'Is there a new flower here?'" recalls Ed. "And I said, 'As a matter of fact,

Erik, there is.' And in front of us, though I hadn't noticed it before, was a whole meadow of beautiful purple flowers."

In 1991 Erik graduated from Boston College with a degree in English and **embarked** on his teaching career. Two years later he moved from Phoenix to Colorado and decided to join a gym. Traveling to the gym by city bus, he got off at a park whose concrete pathways he could navigate alone. When he found those paths obscured by fresh snowfall, Weihenmayer wound up walking into a duck pond. So he returned to the bus stop and tried again. And again. When he finally did reach the gym, it was closed. "Faced with that kind of frustration," he says, "you can look at life as a nightmare or as an adventure. I chose adventure."

In 2001 he became the first and only blind man to summit Everest, a feat that put him on the cover of *Time*. "It's the size of the floor of a one-car garage," Weihenmayer says of the 29,035-foot-high peak. And you should have heard the view from up there. "It's loud," he says, "the sound of sound traveling infinitely through space."

How do you think that sounded?

Weihenmayer's wedding was on Kilimanjaro, with its purple meadows. He met his wife, Ellen, when both were teachers at Phoenix Country Day School. Their workplace romance was revealed at a faculty meeting, when Erik's guide dog, Wizard—who was trained to walk to the first empty chair in the conference room—strode straight over to Ellen, laid his head in her lap and began panting. The room erupted in laughter and applause. The couple now has a five-year-old daughter, Emma.

Talking About the Story

Have students summarize what happened in the article. Why do they think Erik is so successful?

Ask students to describe the qualities they admire about Erik Weihenmayer. Why do they feel this way?

Vocabulary in Action

compel

Before climbing Mount Everest, Erik is compelled to prove that he is blind. If you feel compelled to do something, you feel like you have to do it for some reason.

- Ask what a sick person might feel compelled to do, stay inside and rest or go outside and play. Why?
- Have students describe a time when they were compelled to do something.

preempt

In the article, the sherpa guide preempts Erik from taking out both prosthetic eyes. If one thing preempts another thing, it stops it from happening, often by replacing it.

- Ask students which is an example of preempting, doing their chores before they are told to do them or waiting until they're told before doing the chores. Explain.
- Have students explain how a TV show might be preempted.

endurance

Erik completed a dangerous endurance race called Primal Quest. Endurance is the energy to keep doing something hard for a long time.

- Ask which would need endurance, running for many miles or jogging to the end of the block. Why do you think so?
- Have students describe some situations that require endurance.

superb

In high school, Erik was a superb wrestler. Something that is superb is very, very good.

- Ask which would taste superb, a perfectly made cake or a cake where the cook forgot to add the sugar. Why?
- Have students describe something they are or want to be superb at.

embark

After graduating from college, Erik embarked on his teaching career. If you embark on something new and exciting, you start on it.

- Ask students which a person might embark upon, a trip to the rain forest or a trip to the grocery store.
- Have students name some adventures they would like to embark on.

Words About the Story

fervent

Erik feels strongly about living an adventurous life. You could also say that he is fervent about viewing life as an adventure. Someone who is fervent about something has strong feelings about it.

- Ask students who might be fervent about getting a dog, the girl who begs for a dog every day or the girl who only asks for a dog once. Explain your answer.
- Have students name some things they are fervent about.

acclimate

Erik has had to get used to many new situations. Another way to say that is that he has had to acclimate to them. When you acclimate to a new place or situation, you get used to it.

- Ask who has acclimated quickly, the boy who jumps in the pool and starts swimming around or the boy who jumps in the pool and then just shivers because the water is cold. Why do you think so?
- Have students describe what would help them acclimate to living in a new house.

intuitive

In the story, Erik sensed that there were flowers on the mountain, even though he couldn't see them. You could say he sensed them intuitively. If someone is intuitive, they know things by having a special sense about them, even though they don't have any proof.

- Ask who works more intuitively, an accountant or an artist. Explain your answer.
- Have students give examples of intuitive behavior in people or animals.

Happiness Epidemic

Imagine what it would be like if happiness were a disease spreading across the country, affecting everyone it touched.

Vocabulary

Words From the Poem

These words appear in blue in the poem. Explain these words after the poem is read.

slouch   merriment

stride   reside

invade

Words About the Poem

Explain these words after the poem is read, using context from the poem.

outbreak   droll

symbolic

Getting Ready for the Read-Aloud

Show students the picture on page 159 and read the title aloud. Ask students to notice the white swirls surrounding the children. Point out that the swirls have not yet reached the boy on the bench. Ask students what they think the swirls might be.

Explain that this poem does not rhyme. Explain that not all poems have to rhyme. It is the rhythm and use of language that makes a piece of writing a poem. You might want to explain that this poem contains several metaphors, where the author talks about one thing as if it were something else, (happiness is a disease, a disease is a traveling circus, your heart is a red house, etc.).

There are some words and phrases in the poem that may be new to students. You can briefly explain these expressions as you come to them: *traveling circus,* a circus that goes from town to town to entertain people; *clinically cheerful,* hopelessly happy; *your major organs,* your lungs, stomach, brain, liver, and kidneys; *hearse,* a car used to carry coffins.

Happiness Epidemic

By David Hernandez

Illustrated by Lyuba Bogan

Start dramatically but then voice surprise and then pleasure at the discovery that the disease is actually happiness. End wistfully, as one who wishes the poem were true and happiness so easily achieved.

How would it feel to carry a "bag of misery"?

Without any warning, the disease
sweeps across the country
like a traveling circus.

People who were once blue,
who **slouched** from carrying
a bag of misery over one shoulder

are now clinically cheerful.

Symptoms include kind gestures,
a bouncy **stride**, a smile

bigger than a slice of cantaloupe.
You pray that you will be infected,
hope a happy germ **invades** your body

and multiplies, spreading **merriment**
to all your major organs
like door-to-door Christmas carolers

until the virus finally reaches your heart:
that red house at the end of the block
where your deepest wishes **reside**,

where a dog howls behind a gate
every time that sorrow
pulls his hearse up the driveway.

Talking About
the Poem

Have students tell what they think this poem is about.

Ask students whether they think people can catch happiness from happy people. Why do they think so?

Vocabulary in Action

Words From the Poem

slouch

In the poem, people slouch because they carry a bag of misery over one shoulder. Someone who slouches lets their shoulders and head droop down in a way that doesn't look good.

- Ask students when they would be likely to slouch, when they are very tired or when they are very active. Why do you think so?
- Have students slouch in their chairs.

stride

In the poem, happy people walk with a bouncy stride. Your stride is the way you walk, usually long steps you take when you're walking or running.

- Ask who has a longer stride, a small child or a tall adult. Explain.
- Have students demonstrate different kinds of strides.

invade

Germs can invade people's bodies. If someone invades a place, they enter it rudely or violently.

- Ask what might invade a country, an army or a turkey sandwich. Why is that?
- Have students describe how and why different people or animals invade places.

merriment

The happy germ spreads merriment. When there is merriment, people are having fun and laughing.

- Ask students which place is usually full of merriment, an amusement park or a doctor's office. Why?
- Have students talk about times when they felt a lot of merriment.

reside

In the poem, a person's deepest wishes reside in the heart. If you reside somewhere, you live there or are staying there.

- Ask where a rose bush might reside, in a garden or on a highway. Explain.
- Have students describe the place where they reside.

Vocabulary in Action

outbreak

In the poem, everyone is suddenly very happy. You could say that there is an outbreak of happiness. If there's an outbreak of something, it suddenly starts to show up in many places.

- Ask students which would be an outbreak of song, if everyone in the class suddenly started singing or if everyone sat listening to a song on the radio. Why?
- Have students talk about different ways an outbreak might spread.

symbolic

In the poem, a red house is described as a person's heart. You could say that the red house is symbolic of a heart. Something that is symbolic stands for an idea or thing other than itself.

- Ask what the star-spangled banner is symbolic of, the United States or the planet Earth. Explain.
- Have students describe different symbols and what they stand for.

droll

Many of the ideas and images in this poem are funny. Another way to say that is that they are droll. Something that is droll is funny in a smart way.

- Ask who is more droll, a comedian who tells jokes or a comedian who trips over their own feet. Explain your answer.
- Have students name some books, TV shows, or people that they think are droll.

The Mop Bucket Encore

A Russian immigrant girl describes her relationship with her brother and their new home in the United States as she takes a moment to enjoy her love of music.

Vocabulary

Words From the Story

These words appear in blue in the story. Explain these words after the story is read.

contraption	encore
irresistible	beckon

Words About the Story

Explain these words after the story is read, using context from the story.

mesmerize	avid
perpetual	poignant

Getting Ready for the Read-Aloud

Show students the picture of the girl playing the "cello" on pages 164–165. Read the title aloud. Explain that Sylvie is pretending to play the cello with a mop and bucket. Have students notice the differences and similarities between what is actually happening and what the girl is imagining.

Explain that the United States is a country full of immigrants. Almost everyone is related to an immigrant if they aren't immigrants themselves. An immigrant is someone who moves from the country where they were born to live in a different country. Explain that this story is about a family of immigrants from Russia.

There are some phrases in the story that may be new to students. You can briefly explain these expressions as you come to them: *maestro,* a master of music; *music transports him, just as it transports me,* music seems to take us away from everyday reality; *the Volga,* a river in Russia; *coax,* convince to do something; *the emigration process,* the long process of coming to the United States and becoming a citizen; *stammer,* to speak haltingly or with difficulty.

The Mop Bucket Encore

By Diane L. Burns

Illustrated by Robert Sauber

Bringing the Story to Life

Start the story with the same cheerful, matter-of-fact tone that Sylvie takes with her life. As she allows herself to dream of playing cello infuse your voice with pure pleasure and awe—a perfect dream. Mimic playing a cello. Display shocked horror as Sylvie comes out of her dream and realizes where she is. End with a tone of excited happiness as her dream gets a little closer to being true.

"*S dynom Rajdyenee-ya, Sylvie!*" Still dressed in his janitor's uniform, my big brother, Vlad, greets me in Russian. He hands me a chocolate cupcake with sprinkles pressed into it in the shape of a cello. Then he says in English, "Grandfather sends his love, too."

A small candle in the middle of the cupcake makes me smile. My big brother works two jobs, yet even on this busy Wednesday night, he and Grandfather Sasha have remembered my fifteenth birthday. Vlad will again be late for his night class upstairs, because he's just finished cleaning this high school's hall floors.

Then, because we both love being new American citizens and he loves me more than being on time, he says it again, in English. "Happy birthday, Sylvie." And he adds, "Soon—cello lessons for you."

I hug him, hard. We both know there is no money for cello lessons.

"Go," I tell him. "Turn in your paper on American proverbs."

I pull the cupcake apart and, with one hand, give him half on a napkin while I nudge him with my shoulder toward the stairway. Gratefully, he gulps the treat, and I swallow my half. "Go," I urge him again. But he eyes the big metal bucket on wheels, filled with dirty water, and the mop with its handle sticking up. He hesitates.

"Go," I tell him, one last time. My push is more forceful. "I'll rinse the mop and bucket. I can put them away for you, and they will be safe. The janitor's room locks by itself, re-member? I don't need a key."

With one last, grateful look at me, he grabs his notebook and dashes upstairs. Tonight there will be no time to change back into his regular clothes. I smile again. Vlad loves litera-ture class so much he will not even notice.

Tugging the wheeled bucket with the mop sticking up is not easy, but I manage it. To help Vlad, I've done it before. The only tricky part is not letting the janitor's door spring shut before I am done, so I brace it with the long, thin squee-gee that Vlad uses to clean windows.

And all the time I'm dumping and rinsing, I'm listening. Across the darkened hallway is the music room. Is Maestro Chenko there? Will he play his recordings tonight? If he plays the cello music—my favorite—what a birthday gift that will be!

> Why is Vlad taking classes at night?

I'm wiping the inside of the metal bucket when I hear it: cello music that swells into the air and spills into the quiet hallway. Pulling the bucket by the mop handle, I wheel the **contraption** to the door and listen. I've peeked in before, only to see the maestro conducting passionately in the empty room. Music transports him, just as it transports me. Someday, I think, someday, I will take lessons.

> What do Sylvie and the maestro have in common?

Grandfather's apartment-house neighbor and friend, Mrs. Turner, has been kind enough to show me some basics. A cellist herself, she has even lent me her old instrument to practice on, but it is not a good fit. Mrs. Turner is soft as an armchair, and her cello is very big. I am very small. Still, my arms can just reach around the instrument. However simple, it is music I make.

Around me, the air drips with the sweetness of music. The sound coaxes my fingers. It is **irresistible**.

But how can I play? There is no cello in this place; Mrs. Turner's big one waits for me in Grandfather's apartment. Here there is only this newly cleaned bucket with the mop inside it. Together, in the shadow of this darkened hallway, they have the general shape of a cello, much smaller than Mrs. Turner's. Do I dare to pretend? How can I not? The music is bewitching.

I settle on a stepstool with the bucket between my knees. The mop handle wobbles, but that cannot be helped. Without thinking, I reach for the squeegee, pulling it across the mop handle as my pretend bow.

Too late, I hear the janitor's door click shut. I am locked out, alone in the darkened hallway, with only the mop, bucket, and squeegee. And the music. The enchanting music. Well, the maestro never comes out of his classroom, and Vlad will find me here. His key will open the storage room. I am safe.

The music lifts me like a leaf on the Volga and, swirling, carries me back three years to hazy, painful months in Russia. It lifts me beyond the memory of the fishing accident that took Mama and Papa, the difficulty of getting through the funerals that followed with only Vlad to support me. It pulls me beyond the emigration process and farewell to the familiar, to traveling to America to stay with our one remaining relative. It brings me full circle to joy again, to dear Grandfather Sasha.

Why have Sylvie and her brother come to America?

At last, the music whispers to a close, but I continue to play. It is my own piece now that I hear. One I have made up, an **encore**. Gone is the mop handle; my fingers glide over the cello strings, the squeegee bow creating music so beautiful that it has a soul with a liquid voice.

Eyes closed, I imagine there is a spotlight on me. It shimmers and warms me, and I bask again in the love of family. Seated in the front row beside Vlad and Grandfather Sasha, Mama and Papa are smiling. They have returned to hear me play.

Why do you think Sylvie imagines that she is performing in front of her family?

Too soon, my solo is done, and I open my eyes to find the spotlight full in my face. And then I know: it is no spotlight, just the door to the music room, standing open, with Maestro Chenko in silhouette, staring at me.

No cello. No soaring music. No concert with my family in the front row. Just me, on a stepstool, knees cradling a metal mop bucket. I am again fifteen and untrained. The squeegee falls with a clatter.

Perhaps he will think I am mocking him. But the maestro looks into my eyes and knows the truth. "You must be Sylvie."

He smiles warmly. "Your brother told me to watch for you. He always cleans with such care, does he not? *Tishe yedesh, dalshe budesh.*"

The Russian proverb means, the slower you go, the farther you get. It is one of Grandfather's favorites. Well, Vlad's hectic Wednesday schedule may not fit the proverb. But when it comes to scrubbing floors, or appreciating music, or adjusting to new family, it's true. First in Russia and now in America, Vlad and I continue to learn the great worth of going slowly enough to appreciate what you have.

"Please, come in," Maestro Chenko says, **beckoning** to me with his conductor's wand.

The room is round and bright. What a wide, inviting space waiting to be filled with the music that his students will make tomorrow!

Then I see it. In a corner of the room, a small cello, just my size, leans on its stand.

At the sight of the cello, I clasp my hands together. I cannot help it.

The maestro pulls the wondrous cello into the middle of the room and arranges a chair in position. He nods toward me, then the chair. He wants me to sit in it? To play? No, I couldn't!

"But . . . but . . . ," I stammer, my cheeks flaming red, "it was pretend."

Maestro Chenko points to the wheeled bucket still trailing along behind me. His smile deepens, and he says gently, "In an empty hallway, you play the music that swirls inside your heart. I conduct in an empty room the music that fills my own. We each have a secret, yes?"

> Why do Sylvie and her brother think it's important to "go slowly"?

My cheeks flame deeper.

"My friend Vlad is right," he says with a kindly smile. "You have a passion to make music. So, on Wednesday nights—while Vlad studies upstairs and you and I both long to be carried by music—perhaps you will let me listen as you make melodies on this little instrument?"

Vlad, remarkable Vlad, has arranged this with the maestro!

"*Balsho-yeh spaseeba,*" I whisper. "Thank you very much."

I settle into position at the cello that fits as if it were made for me. I draw the bow across the strings, making music that tells of this surprising birthday night. It tells, too, of the trip from my old home in Russia to Grandfather's love and the maestro's cello lessons in America. It is a memorable journey, is it not, when music is the road?

Talking About the Story

Have students summarize what happened in the story and ask if they were happy with how the story ended.

Ask students to think about how Sylvie feels about music. Have them share things they feel that way about.

Words From the Story

contraption

Sylvie calls the bucket with mop a contraption. If you call a thing a contraption, you think it's complicated or strange, and you don't understand it or like it very much.

- Ask which is a contraption, a computer that keeps on freezing or a simple wooden desk. Explain why.
- Have students give some examples of contraptions.

irresistible

In the story, the cello music has an irresistible affect on Sylvie's fingers, making them want to play. If something is irresistible, you are unable to fight against it.

- Ask students what they might find irresistible, an urge to pull their little sister's ponytail or an urge to sit quietly and do their homework. Why?
- Have students demonstrate how they might react when they see an irresistible cupcake.

encore

When Sylvie is "playing the cello" with the mop and bucket, she decides to play an encore. An encore is a short, extra performance done at the end of a longer performance because the audience asks for more.

- Ask students where they would be more likely to see an encore, in a concert hall or in a movie theater. Why is that?
- Ask students if they have ever heard people call for an encore at the end of a really good performance.

beckon

In the story, the maestro beckons to Sylvie with his conductor's wand to come into the music room. If you beckon to someone, you signal that you want them to come to you.

- Ask who is beckoning, the girl who waves at her friend to join her or the girl who waves a friend away because she's busy. Explain your answer.
- Have students take turns beckoning each other across the room.

Vocabulary in Action

mesmerize

Sylvie forgets everything she is supposed to be doing when she hears the wonderful cello music. You could also say that she is mesmerized by the music. If you are mesmerized by something, it is so amazing that you can't think of or watch anything else.

- Ask students what might mesmerize them, a large aquarium filled with quick colorful fish or an empty school hallway. Explain why that is.
- Have students tell about a time they were mesmerized by something.

perpetual

Sylvie always desires to play the cello, even when it's not possible. You could also say that she has a perpetual desire to play. If something is perpetual, it goes on forever.

- Ask which is perpetual, gravity or the flight of a paper airplane. Explain your answer.
- Have students give examples of things that are, or seem to be, perpetual.

avid

Sylvie is very excited and enthusiastic about the cello. You could also say that she is an avid cello player. If someone is avid about something they do, they are very enthusiastic about it.

- Ask who is avid, the boy who buys every CD of a music group as soon as it comes out or the boy who just enjoys the music when it's on the radio. Why?
- Ask students to talk about things they are avid about.

poignant

Hearing the cello music reminds Sylvie of her family back in Russia and brings memories of her dead parents. You could also say that the cello music affected her in a poignant way. Something that is poignant affects your feelings so much that it makes you a little sad.

- Ask students which would likely be more poignant, watching old home-movies of themselves as a baby or playing the newest video game. Why is that?
- Have students give examples of things they think are poignant.

GLOBAL TREASURE HUNT

LESSON
21

This article discusses a growing sport called geocaching, in which anyone with a global positioning system (GPS) can go in search of hidden treasures left behind by other geocachers.

Vocabulary

Words From the Story

These words appear in blue in the story. Explain these words after the story is read.

restricted   **meld**

stash   **consult**

Words About the Story

Explain these words after the story is read, using context from the story.

gadget   **surmise**

scout   **plausible**

Getting Ready for the Read-Aloud

Show students the picture of the children with the GPS unit on page 174 and read the title aloud. Explain that the device the girl is holding is called a GPS unit and that the kids are using it to find hidden treasure. Have students notice the excited expressions on the faces of the kids.

Explain to students that GPS stands for Global Positioning System. Then tell them that the GPS unit has a screen that shows users where they are on the planet using latitude and longitude coordinates. These sets of numbers tell a place's distance north or south of the Equator and east or west of the Prime Meridian. Ask students to share what they know about latitude and longitude coordinates.

There are some words in the story that may be new to students. You might wish to briefly explain these words and phrases as you come to them: *booty,* prize or treasure; *conventional locales,* ordinary places; *accurate,* exactly correct; *civilian,* person who is not in the military; *capability,* what they should be able to do; *transcends,* that goes beyond the limits of.

GLOBAL TREASURE HUNT

By Brian Handwerk

Illustrated by Doris Ettlinger

The idea of hunting for treasure is exciting to most children, so read the article in an enthusiastic tone of voice. Give special emphasis to the line "Interested? There's a cache near you." Later, use an awed tone of voice when you read "Caches could be hidden on sheer cliffs, requiring climbing gear, or found in the underwater realm of scuba divers."

The key to hidden treasure lies in your handheld GPS (global positioning system) unit. GPS-based "geocaching" is a high-tech sport being played by thousands of people across the globe.

To the uninitiated, the sight of people circling methodically around a local woodland or city park, GPS device in hand, is a bit puzzling. But this strange behavior has a purpose: They're people in search of a cache—one of tens of thousands of hidden treasures planted by other players.

"I go out with my five-year-old and nine-year-old as a family," said geocacher Rich Ness, assistant manager of a Bloomington, Minnesota outdoor-gear store (GPS coordinates: latitude 44° 51.6' N, longitude 93° 17.3' W). "I haven't come across a kid yet who didn't think it's the greatest thing ever."

Adults are hooked too.

Interested? There's a cache near you. In fact you might be amazed at just how many caches are near you.

But just what is a cache? The answer is as different as the people who hide them.

The cache, often a piece of Tupperware, might contain only a logbook with some amusing stories of geocaching adventure. Others are stocked with prizes like books, software, CDs, videos, money, or toys. (Food is frowned upon, as are such **restricted** items as alcohol and fireworks.)

What would you hide in a cache?

Cache hiders use one of several Internet hosting sites to publish and share the coordinates of their clue sites, or waypoint. Players choose a target, then set off with handheld GPS units —using the technology to locate a variety of hidden booty.

"People have gotten very creative," said Quinn George Stone, a resident of Rochester, New York, and a founder of hosting site Navicache.com. "The first coordinates might take you to a monument or a gravestone with dates on it, where you might have to do some mathematical equations to get the next set of coordinates. Some caches actually have 30 to 40 waypoints before you get to the container."

A few basic rules apply when one successfully finds a cache: Take something from it, leave something in it, and fill out the logbook to document your adventure.

Why should you leave something in the cache?

It may sound easy to follow a GPS unit to known coordinates, but getting there is not always so simple.

Caches could be hidden on sheer cliffs, requiring climbing gear, or found in the underwater realm of scuba divers. Urban caches are **stashed** inside and outside buildings. While most caches are located in far more conventional locales and require only walking, your GPS device will only take you so far before your brain must take over.

"It's a lot of fun, and if the GPS units were more accurate, it wouldn't be as much fun," geocacher Ed Hall said. "GPS gets you within 20 feet (6 meters), but then you turn it off and start looking under logs and behind bushes to find who knows what."

Why might it not be as fun if the GPS units were more accurate?

Hall's Colorado-based Buxley's Geocaching Waypoint Web site features roughly 1,500 maps that display where caches can be found around the globe.

It's not known if former U.S. President Bill Clinton has attempted geocaching, but his administration gave the sport its start by ending GPS Selective Availability (SA) on May 1, 2000. SA was a degradation feature that limited the accuracy of civilian-owned GPS units to one-tenth their capability.

Today GPS devices are widely available and increasingly popular among boaters, hikers, and other outdoor enthusiasts. Units range in price from U.S. $100 to $1,000.

"Geocaching has helped introduce GPS technology to the masses and to reach a younger audience," said Pete Brumbaugh, a spokesperson for a leading manufacturer of handheld GPS devices. "There are schools that use geocaching to teach geography, to **meld** technology and the outdoors together," he said.

Ness, who's seen increased interest in geocaching at his store, sees a common bond that transcends age or occupation. "Most people just like to be outdoors," Ness said. "This is a reason to go for a hike or a walk or go to and find that new park somewhere."

Indeed, geocaching has been one of the best tour guides Ed Hall has ever **consulted**.

"People tend to put caches in beautiful places that they've visited," he said. "My boys and I geocache when traveling, and locals have directed us to some of the most beautiful spots around the country that we never would have found."

Talking About the Story

Have students share what they learned about geocaching.

Ask students to tell why they would or would not want to try geocaching.

Words From the Story

restricted

In the article, fireworks and alcohol are restricted from being used in caches. If something is restricted, it is limited to a certain place, size, or group of people.

- Ask what is restricted, having paper in school or having pets in school. Why do you think so?
- Have students give examples of other things that are restricted.

stash

People have been known to stash caches inside and outside buildings. If you stash something, you put it in a safe, secret place.

- Ask who is stashing something, a man who leaves his money on a table or a man who locks his money in a safe. Why?
- Have students name places in the classroom where they could stash a CD.

meld

In the article, someone talks about how geocaching melds technology and the outdoors. If you meld two or more things, you combine them or blend them together.

- Ask students which is an example of melding, pulling apart a piece of clay or pressing two pieces of clay together. Explain.
- Have students meld their hands by interlocking their fingers.

consult

In the article, someone says that geocaching is one of the best tour guides they have ever consulted. If you consult someone, you get advice or information from them.

- Ask students what they would be more likely to consult, their parents or a saxophone. Explain your answer.
- Have students tell who they might consult if they wanted to find the author of a particular book.

Vocabulary in Action

Words About the Story

gadget

Geocachers use a GPS unit to find caches. You could say that the GPS unit is a kind of gadget. A gadget is a small machine or device that does something useful.

- Ask students which is a gadget, a box of tissues or a cell phone. Explain why.
- Have students tell what gadgets they would like to have.

scout

The article says that GPS units will get you within twenty feet of a cache, and then you might need to look under logs and behind bushes to find it. In other words, you might need to scout for the treasure. If you scout for something, you search for it, often in a certain area.

- Ask who is scouting, a detective looking around a neighborhood for a missing person or a girl jumping rope in the woods. Explain your answer.
- Have students scout the classroom for things that are green.

surmise

Geocachers can only guess what might be in a cache. In other words, they surmise what might be in the cache. If you surmise something, you guess that it's true based on what you know, but you don't know for sure.

- Ask who is surmising, someone who performs a scientific experiment or someone who predicts what might happen in a scientific experiment. Why do you think so?
- Have students surmise your height.

plausible

After they reach the coordinates of a cache, geocachers search the most likely places that a cache may be hidden. You could say that they search the most plausible places. If you say something is plausible, you think that it could reasonably be true.

- Ask which is more plausible, a story about a girl with ten arms or a story about a boy who spends a week with his cousins. Why?
- Have students give you a plausible excuse for being late to class.

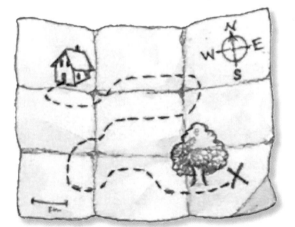

La Bamba

In this humorous story, a mishap that at first seems embarrassing makes a boy's performance at a talent show a rousing success.

Vocabulary

Words From the Story

These words appear in blue in the story. Explain these words after the story is read.

yearn	verge
limelight	mingle
flail	

Words About the Story

Explain these words after the story is read, using context from the story.

feign	miserable
incessant	

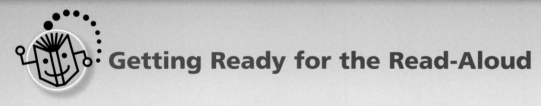

Getting Ready for the Read-Aloud

Show students the picture of the boy onstage on page 181 and read the title aloud. Explain that the boy is performing for his family and friends. Have them notice the expressions on the faces of people in the audience.

Explain that this is a story about a boy who gets up the courage to enter a school talent show. Then tell students that the song he pretends to sing is by Ritchie Valens, the first Mexican-American rock star, who was popular during the 1950s. The song, "La Bamba," is based on a traditional Mexican song of the same name. You may

also want to mention that before there were CDs, people listened to music on records. Records are discs marked with grooves. Record players use a needle to play records. The needle can sometimes get stuck or skip across the grooves if the record has been scratched.

The following terms can be explained as you come to them: *pantomime,* act without speaking; *forty-five record,* type of record; *"Para bailar la bamba,"* "To dance the bamba;" *cue,* signal to do something; *"Ah, que niños tan truchas,"* "Ah, these children are really smart."

La Bamba

from *Baseball in April and Other Stories*

By Gary Soto

Illustrated by
Stacey Schuett

Manuel was the fourth of seven children and looked like a lot of kids in his neighborhood: black hair, brown face, and skinny legs scuffed from summer play. But summer was giving way to fall: The trees were turning red, the lawns brown, and the pomegranate trees were heavy with fruit. Manuel walked to school in the frosty morning, kicking leaves and thinking of tomorrow's talent show. He was still amazed that he had volunteered. He was going to pretend to sing Ritchie Valens's "La Bamba" before the entire school.

Why did I raise my hand? he asked himself, but in his heart he knew the answer. He **yearned** for the **limelight**. He wanted applause as loud as a thunderstorm and to hear his friends say, "Man, that was bad!" And he wanted to impress the girls, especially Petra Lopez, the second-prettiest girl in his class. The prettiest was already taken by his friend Ernie. Manuel knew he should be reasonable since he himself was not great-looking, just average.

Manuel kicked through the fresh-fallen leaves. When he got to school, he realized he had forgotten his math workbook. If the teacher found out, he would have to stay after school and miss practice for the talent show. But fortunately for him, they did drills that morning.

During lunch Manuel hung around with Benny, who was also in the talent show. Benny was going to play the trumpet in spite of the fat lip he had gotten playing football.

"How do I look?" Manuel asked. He cleared his throat and started moving his lips in pantomime. No words came out, just a hiss that sounded like a snake. Manuel tried to look emotional, **flailing** his arms on the high notes and opening his eyes and mouth as wide as he could when he came to *"Para bailar la baaaaammmba."*

After Manuel finished, Benny said it looked all right but suggested Manuel dance while he sang. Manuel thought for a moment and decided it was a good idea.

"Yeah, just think you're like Michael Jackson or someone like that," Benny suggested. "But don't get carried away."

During rehearsal, Mr. Roybal, nervous about his debut as the school's talent coordinator, [was upset] when the lever that controlled the speed on the record player jammed.

"Darn," he growled, trying to force the lever. "What's wrong with you?"

"Is it broken?" Manuel asked, bending over for a closer look. It looked all right to him.

Mr. Roybal assured Manuel that he would have a good record player at the talent show, even if it meant bringing his own stereo from home.

Manuel sat in a folding chair, twirling his record on his thumb. He watched a skit about personal hygiene, a mother-and-daughter violin duo, five first-grade girls jumping rope, a karate kid breaking boards, three girls singing, and a skit about the pilgrims. If the record player hadn't been broken, he would have gone after the karate kid, an easy act to follow, he told himself.

As he twirled his forty-five record, Manuel thought they had a great talent show. The entire school would be amazed. His mother and father would be proud, and his brothers and sisters would be jealous and pout. It would be a night to remember.

Benny walked onto the stage, raised his trumpet to his mouth, and waited for his cue. Mr. Roybal raised his hand like a symphony conductor and let it fall dramatically. Benny inhaled and blew so loud that Manuel dropped his record, which rolled across the cafeteria floor until it hit a wall. Manuel raced after it, picked it up, and wiped it clean.

> Do you think Manuel's record is all right?

"Boy, I'm glad it didn't break," he said with a sigh.

That night Manuel had to do the dishes and a lot of homework, so he could only practice in the shower. In bed he prayed that he wouldn't mess up. He prayed that it wouldn't be like when he was a first-grader. For Science Week he had wired together a C battery and a bulb and told everyone he had discovered how a flashlight worked. He was so pleased with himself that he practiced for hours pressing the wire to the battery, making the bulb wink a dim, orangish light. He showed it to so many kids in his neighborhood that when it was time to show his class how a flashlight worked, the battery was dead. He pressed the wire to the battery, but the bulb didn't respond. He pressed until his thumb hurt and some kids in the back started snickering.

But Manuel fell asleep confident that nothing would go wrong this time.

The next morning his father and mother beamed at him. They were proud that he was going to be in the talent show.

"I wish you would tell us what you're doing," his mother said. His father, a pharmacist who wore a blue smock with his name on a plastic rectangle, looked up from the newspaper and sided with his wife. "Yes, what are you doing in the talent show?"

"You'll see," Manuel said, with his mouth full of cereal.

The day whizzed by, and so did his afternoon chores and dinner. Suddenly he was dressed in his best clothes and standing next to Benny backstage, listening to the commotion as the cafeteria filled with school kids and parents. The lights dimmed, and Mr. Roybal, sweaty in a tight suit and a necktie with a large knot, wet his lips and parted the stage curtains.

"Good evening, everyone," the kids behind the curtain heard him say. "Good evening to you," some of the smart-alecky kids said back to him.

"Tonight we bring you the best John Burroughs Elementary has to offer, and I'm sure that you'll be both pleased and amazed that our little school houses so much talent. And now, without further ado, let's get on with the show." He turned and, with a swish of his hand, commanded, "Part the curtain." The curtains parted in jerks. A girl dressed as a toothbrush and a boy dressed as a dirty gray tooth walked onto the stage and sang:

Brush, brush, brush

Floss, floss, floss

Gargle the germs away—hey! hey! hey!

After they finished singing, they turned to Mr. Roybal, who dropped his hand. The toothbrush dashed around the stage after the dirty tooth, which was laughing and having a great time until it slipped and nearly rolled off the stage.

Mr. Roybal jumped out and caught it just in time. "Are you OK?"

The dirty tooth answered, "Ask my dentist," which drew laughter and applause from the audience.

The violin duo played next, and except for one time when the girl got lost, they sounded fine. People applauded, and some even stood up. Then the first-grade girls maneuvered onto the stage while jumping rope. They were all smiles and bouncing ponytails as a hundred cameras flashed at once. Mothers "awhed" and fathers sat up proudly.

The karate kid was next. He did a few kicks, yells, and chops, and finally, when his father held up a board, punched it in two. The audience clapped and looked at each other, wide-eyed with respect. The boy bowed to the audience, and father and son ran off the stage.

Manuel remained behind the stage, shivering with fear. He mouthed the words to "La Bamba" and swayed left to right. Why did he raise his hand and volunteer? Why couldn't he have just sat there like the rest of the kids and not said anything? While the karate kid was onstage, Mr. Roybal, more sweaty than before, took Manuel's forty-five record and placed it on a new record player.

Does Manuel want to go on stage?

"You ready?" Mr. Roybal asked.

"Yeah . . ."

Mr. Roybal walked back on stage and announced that Manuel Gomez, a fifth-grader in Mrs. Knight's class, was going to pantomime Ritchie Valens's classic hit "La Bamba."

The cafeteria roared with applause. Manuel was nervous but loved the noisy crowd. He pictured his mother and father applauding loudly and his brothers and sister also clapping, though not as energetically.

Manuel walked on stage and the song started immediately. Glassy-eyed from the shock of being in front of so many people, Manuel moved his lips and swayed in a made-up dance step. He couldn't see his parents, but he could see his brother Mario, who was a year younger, thumb-wrestling with a friend. Mario was wearing Manuel's favorite shirt; he would deal with Mario later. He saw some other kids get up and head for the drinking fountain, and a baby sitting in the middle of an aisle sucking her thumb and watching him intently.

What am I doing here? thought Manuel. This is no fun at all. Everyone was just sitting there. Some people were moving to the beat, but most were just watching him, like they would a monkey at the zoo.

But when Manuel did a fancy dance step, there was a burst of applause and some girls screamed. Manuel tried another dance step. He heard more applause and screams and started getting into the groove as he shivered and snaked like Michael Jackson around the stage. But the record got stuck, and he had to sing

Para bailar la bamba

Para bailar la bamba

Para bailar la bamba

Para bailar la bamba

again and again.

Manuel couldn't believe his bad luck. The audience began to laugh and stand up in their chairs. Manuel remembered how the forty-five record had dropped from his hand and rolled across the cafeteria floor. It probably got scratched, he thought, and now it was stuck, and he was stuck dancing and moving his lips to the same words over and over. He had never been so embarrassed. He would have to ask his parents to move the family out of town.

Why is Manuel embarrassed?

After Mr. Roybal ripped the needle across the record, Manuel slowed his dance steps to a halt. He didn't know what to do except bow to the audience, which applauded wildly, and scoot off the stage, on the **verge** of tears. This was worse than the homemade flashlight. At least no one laughed then; they just snickered.

Manuel stood alone, trying hard to hold back the tears as Benny, center stage, played his trumpet. Manuel was jealous because he sounded great, then mad as he recalled that it was Benny's loud trumpet playing that made the forty-five record fly out of his hands. But when the entire cast lined up for a curtain call, Manuel received a burst of applause that was so loud it shook the walls of the cafeteria. Later, as he **mingled** with the kids and parents, everyone patted him on the shoulder and told him, "Way to go. You were really funny."

Funny? Manuel thought. Did he do something funny?

Funny. Crazy. Hilarious. These were the words people said to him. He was confused but beyond caring. All he knew was that people were paying attention to him, and his brother and sisters looked at him with a mixture of jealousy and awe. He was going to pull Mario aside and punch him in the arm for wearing his shirt, but he cooled it. He was enjoying the limelight. A teacher brought him cookies and punch, and the popular kids who had never before given him the time of day now clustered around him. Ricardo, the editor of the school bulletin, asked him how he made the needle stick.

Why is everyone treating Manuel like a star?

"It just happened," Manuel said, crunching on a star-shaped cookie.

At home that night his father, eager to undo the buttons on his shirt and ease into his La-Z-Boy recliner, asked Manuel the same thing, how he managed to make the song stick on the words *"Para bailar la bamba."*

Manuel thought quickly and reached for scientific jargon he had read in magazines. "Easy, Dad. I used laser tracking with high optics and low functional decibels per channel." His proud but confused father told him to be quiet and go to bed.

"Ah, *que niños tan truchas,*" he said as he walked to the kitchen for a glass of milk. "I don't know how you kids nowadays get so smart."

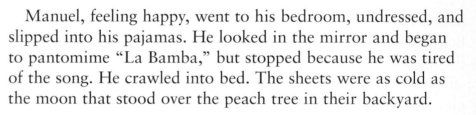

Manuel, feeling happy, went to his bedroom, undressed, and slipped into his pajamas. He looked in the mirror and began to pantomime "La Bamba," but stopped because he was tired of the song. He crawled into bed. The sheets were as cold as the moon that stood over the peach tree in their backyard.

He was relieved that the day was over. Next year, when they asked for volunteers for the talent show, he wouldn't raise his hand. Probably.

Why didn't Manuel tell his father the truth?

Talking About the Story

Have students tell what happened when Manuel performed on-stage. Then ask them to discuss how Manuel feels about all the attention he gets.

Ask students to talk about a time when they or a friend learned from or were helped by an embarrassing moment.

Vocabulary in Action

yearn

In the story, Manuel yearns for the applause of an audience. If you yearn for something, you want it very much.

- Ask students what someone would yearn for, a stomachache or relief from the pain of a stomachache. Why?
- Have students tell what things they yearn for.

limelight

Manuel volunteers for the talent show because he wants to be in the limelight. If you are in the limelight, you are getting a lot of public attention.

- Ask students who is in the limelight, a famous comedian or someone who works in a quiet office. Why do you think so?
- Have students name some people who are in the limelight.

flail

When Manuel practices his performance in front of Benny, he flails his arms. Something that is flailing is waving around wildly.

- Ask students who flails, someone laying on a couch or someone on skates who just lost their balance. Explain your answer.
- Have students pretend to flail a rope.

verge

Manuel scoots off the stage on the verge of tears. If you are on the verge of something, you are about to do it or ready to do it.

- Ask students which person is on the verge, a runner who is waiting for the starting signal to go off or a runner who has just finished a race. Explain.
- Have students describe a time when they were on the verge of laughter.

mingle

After the talent show, Manuel mingles with the other kids and their parents. If people or things mingle, they mix together and interact with each other.

- Ask when a person might mingle, during a moment of silence or at a school dance. Explain why.
- Have students mingle briefly.

Vocabulary in Action

feign

In the story, Manuel pretends to sing. In other words, he feigns the ability to sing. If you feign something, you pretend to feel it or do it.

- Ask who is feigning, someone who plays a queen on television or the Queen of England. Explain why.
- Have students tell about a time that they feigned something.

incessant

In the story, the record player keeps playing one part of the song over and over. Another way to say that is that it plays one part of the song incessantly. Something that is incessant keeps happening and never stops.

- Ask which is incessant, a motorcycle that whizzes past your house one day or a bug that seems to buzz in your ear wherever you go. Explain your answer.
- Have students describe a time when someone bothered them incessantly.

miserable

Manuel leaves the stage feeling depressed. In other words, he is miserable. If someone or something is miserable, they are very unhappy or they make you feel very unhappy.

- Ask which would make you feel miserable, staying warm by the fire on a dark and stormy night or having to walk across town on a dark and stormy night. Why?
- Have students practice looking miserable.

The Mysterious Mr. Lincoln

Some say that a picture is worth a thousand words, but is it really? This story explores the many faces of Abraham Lincoln, who was the most photographed man of his time.

Vocabulary

Words From the Story

These words appear in blue in the story. Explain these words after the story is read.

lean	**reticent**
listless	**magnitude**
animation	

Words About the Story

Explain these words after the story is read, using context from the story.

conspicuous	**gregarious**
esteem	

Getting Ready for the Read-Aloud

Show students the picture of President Abraham Lincoln on page 192 and read the title aloud. Have them describe how Lincoln looks and ask why this story might be titled "The Mysterious Mr. Lincoln."

Point out that people in old photos rarely smiled. Explain that photography was a new science when Lincoln was president of the United States. Explain that Lincoln was president during the Civil War, a war in the United States where the southern states tried to become their own country, and the northern and southern states fought against each other. One of the results of the war was making slavery illegal.

The following phrases occur in the story and can be briefly explained as you come to them: *homely*, plain; *two-faced*, someone who acts differently with different people; *countenance*, face; *made good*, became successful; *eloquent*, very good with words; *yarns*, stories; *denounce*, speak against; *paramount*, main; *abolitionist*, someone who acts against slavery; *dismemberment*, taking something apart; *survey*, look over.

The Mysterious Mr. Lincoln

from *Lincoln: A Photobiography*
By Russell Freedman

President Abraham Lincoln once said, "If any personal description of me is thought desirable, it may be said, I am, in height, six feet, four inches, nearly; **lean** in flesh, weighing, on average, one hundred and eighty pounds; dark complexion, with course black hair and grey eyes—no other marks or brands recollected."

Abraham Lincoln wasn't the sort of man who could lose himself in a crowd. After all, he stood six feet four inches tall, and to top it off, he wore a high silk hat.

His height was mostly in his long bony legs. When he sat in a chair, he seemed no taller than anyone else. It was only when he stood up that he towered above other men.

Use different tones (humorous, serious, intellectual, etc.) as appropriate when reading about different aspects of Lincoln's personality or history. Pay special attention to punctuation in quoted matter, as those sentences tend to be long and complicated.

Is that a good description of how Lincoln looks?

At first glance, most people thought he was homely. Lincoln thought so too, referring once to his "poor, lean, lank face." As a young man he was sensitive about his gawky looks, but in time, he learned to laugh at himself. When a rival called him "two-faced" during a political debate, Lincoln replied: "I leave it to my audience. If I had another face, do you think I'd wear this one?"

According to those who knew him, Lincoln was a man of many faces. In repose, he often seemed sad and gloomy. But when he began to speak, his expression changed. "The dull, **listless** features dropped like a mask," said a Chicago newspaperman. "The eyes began to sparkle, the mouth to smile, the whole countenance was wreathed in **animation**, so that a stranger would have said, 'Why, this man, so angular and solemn a moment ago, is really handsome!'"

Lincoln was the most photographed man of his time, but his friends insisted that no photo ever did him justice. It's no wonder. Back then, cameras required long exposures. The person being photographed had to "freeze" as the seconds ticked by. If he blinked an eye, the picture would be blurred. That's why Lincoln looks so stiff and formal in his photos. We never see him laughing or joking.

Can you imagine having to stay perfectly still for a whole minute just to get one photo?

Artists and writers tried to capture the "real" Lincoln that the camera missed, but something about the man always escaped them. His changeable features, his tones, gestures, and expressions, seemed to defy description.

Today it's hard to imagine Lincoln as he really was. And he never cared to reveal much about himself. In company he was witty and talkative, but he rarely betrayed his inner feelings. According to William Herndon, his law partner, he was "the most secretive—**reticent**—shut-mouthed man that ever lived."

In his own time, Lincoln was never fully understood even by his closest friends. Since then, his story has been told and retold so many times, he has become as much a legend as a flesh-and-blood human being. While the legend is based on truth, it is only partly true. And it hides the man behind it like a disguise.

The legendary Lincoln is known as Honest Abe, a humble man of the people who rose from a log cabin to the White House. There's no doubt that Lincoln was a poor boy who made good. And it's true that he carried his folksy manners and homespun speech to the White House with him. He said "howdy" to visitors and invited them to "stay a spell." He greeted diplomats while wearing carpet slippers, called his wife "mother" at receptions, and told bawdy jokes at cabinet meetings.

Does this sound like the same man in the picture?

Lincoln may have seemed like a common man, but he wasn't. His friends agreed that he was one of the most ambitious people they had ever known. Lincoln struggled hard to rise above his log-cabin origins, and he was proud of his achievements. By the time he ran for president he was a wealthy man, earning a large income from his law practice and his many investments. As for the nickname Abe, he hated it. No one who knew him well ever called him Abe to his face. They addressed him as Lincoln or Mr. Lincoln.

Lincoln is often described as a sloppy dresser, careless about his appearance. In fact, he patronized the best tailor in Springfield, Illinois, buying two suits a year. That was at a time when many men lived, died, and were buried in the same suit.

It's true that Lincoln had little formal "eddication," as he would have pronounced it. Almost everything he "larned" he taught himself. All his life he said "thar" for *there*, "git" for *get*, "kin" for *can*. Even so, he became an eloquent public speaker who could hold a vast audience spellbound, and a great writer whose finest phrases still ring in our ears. He was known to sit up late into the night, discussing Shakespeare's plays with White House visitors.

He was certainly a humorous man, famous for his rollicking stories. But he was also moody and melancholy, tormented by long and frequent bouts of depression. Humor was his therapy. He relied on his yarns, a friend observed, to "whistle down sadness."

He had a cool, logical mind, trained in the courtroom, and a practical, commonsense approach to problems. Yet he was deeply superstitious, a believer in dreams, omens, and visions.

We admire Lincoln today as an American folk hero. During the Civil War, however, he was the most unpopular president the nation had ever known. His critics called him a tyrant, a hick, a stupid baboon who was unfit for his office. As commander in chief of the armed forces, he was denounced as a bungling amateur who meddled in military affairs he knew nothing about. But he also had his supporters.

They praised him as a farsighted statesman, a military master-mind who engineered the Union victory.

Lincoln is best known as the Great Emancipator, the man who freed the slaves. Yet he did not enter the war with that idea in mind. "My paramount object in this struggle is to save the Union," he said in 1862, "and is *not* either to save or destroy slavery." As the war continued, Lincoln's attitude changed. Eventually he came to regard the conflict as a moral crusade to wipe out the sin of slavery.

No black leader was more critical of Lincoln than the fiery abolitionist writer and editor Frederick Douglass. Douglass had grown up as a slave. He had won his freedom by escaping to the North. Early in the war, impatient with Lincoln's cautious leadership, Douglass called him "preeminently the white man's president, entirely devoted to the welfare of white men." Later, Douglass changed his mind and came to admire Lincoln. Several years after the war, he said this about the sixteenth president:

"His greatest mission was to accomplish two things: first, to save his country from dismemberment and ruin; and, second, to free his country from the great crime of slavery. . . . taking him for all in all, measuring the tremendous **magnitude** of the work before him, considering the necessary means to ends, and surveying the end from the beginning, infinite wisdom has seldom sent any man into the world better fitted for his mission than Abraham Lincoln."

Talking About the Story

Have students discuss what they learned from this story.

Ask students if they think a photograph of them shows who they really are.

Vocabulary in Action

Words From the Story

lean

In the story, Abraham Lincoln was described as tall and lean. Someone or something that is lean is thin and doesn't have a lot of extra fat or weight.

- Ask which dog is lean, a bulldog or a greyhound. Explain.
- Have students name some other people or animals who are lean.

listless

Lincoln's expression looked listless when he was resting. If you are listless, you have no energy and don't feel like doing anything.

- Ask students when they might look listless, when they're excited about going to a friend's house or when they're bored and can't think of anything to do. Why do you think so?
- Have students sit in their chairs or walk around in a listless fashion.

animation

The author explains that when Lincoln began to speak, his expression became animated. Someone with animation is lively in the way they act or speak.

- Ask students who might be speaking with animation, the girl who's describing her wonderful weekend or the girl who's reading aloud a number from a phone book. Explain your answer.
- Have students say "the king eats waffles," first without animation and then with animation.

reticent

In the story, Lincoln is reticent about sharing personal information. If you are reticent, you are shy and do not like to share your thoughts and feelings with others.

- Ask who is reticent, a person who tells everyone everything or a person who keeps a secret. Why is that?
- Have students think of a person they know who is reticent and a person who is the opposite of reticent.

magnitude

Fredrick Douglass said that keeping the United States together was a job of great magnitude. The magnitude of something is its large size or importance.

- Ask which has magnitude, an earthquake or a raindrop. Explain.
- Have students brainstorm historical events that had magnitude.

Vocabulary in Action

conspicuous

When Lincoln stood next to other people, his height was very obvious. Another way to describe his height is to say it was conspicuous. If something or someone is conspicuous, they stick out and are very obvious.

- Ask students what is conspicuous at night, bright, reflective colors or dark colors. Why?
- Have students look around the classroom to find things that are conspicuous, and then have them look more closely for things that are not conspicuous, or are inconspicuous.

esteem

Many people admire Abraham Lincoln. You might also say that they hold Lincoln in esteem. If you feel esteem for someone, you admire and respect them.

- Ask students who they are more likely to feel esteem for, their role model or someone they don't like. Why is that?
- Have students name people for whom they feel esteem.

gregarious

According to the author, Lincoln was happiest when he was around other people. You could also say that he was gregarious. If you are gregarious, you enjoy being with other people.

- Ask who is more likely to be gregarious, a boy who joins a lot of clubs and after school activites or a boy who doesn't do any of that. Explain.
- Have students talk about when they feel gregarious and when they don't.

from The Color of Water

In this true story, a young boy must learn to face his fears of going to school and coming home by himself.

Vocabulary

Words From the Story

These words appear in blue in the story. Explain these words after the story is read.

quip   subside

attire   intent

Words About the Story

Explain these words after the story is read, using context from the story.

burden   solace

foreboding   heed

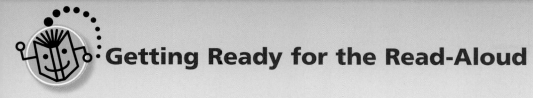 Getting Ready for the Read-Aloud

Show students the picture of the boy who has just gotten off the school bus on pages 200–201 and read the title aloud. Explain that there is no one there to meet him and he does not know how to get home. Have them notice his confused expression.

The first paragraph in this story paints a picture of a family in which the mother has a special way of teaching her 12 children about life. Explain that her system may seem cruel to some but ask students to listen and see what they think of the lesson the mother teaches her son.

Explain that this true story is about a boy who is just starting school and is afraid to be without his mother. Then tell them this story takes place in the 1960s in a primarily African-American neighborhood. At this time, there was still segregation. If necessary, explain that the boy's mother is Caucasian and his father is African American.

The following words and phrases can be explained as you come to them: *kill or be killed*, take care of yourself; *left to your own devices*, left to take care of things on your own; *guffaws*, big laughs.

from

The Color of Water

By James McBride

Illustrated by
Marni Backer

Begin reading the
story using a worried
tone of voice. When
you reach "Surprise
reward," you should
start to sound more
at ease. At the end
of the story, you may
want to read the first
two sentences again
to show students that
this story was about
Mommy wanting her
son to be strong and
self-sufficient.

It was kill or be killed in my house, and Mommy understood that, in fact created the system. You were left to your
own devices or so you thought until you were at your very
wits' end, at which time she would step in and rescue you.

This sounds like an
interesting family! Let's
find out what happens.

I was terrified when it came my turn to go to school. Although P.S. 118 was only eight blocks away, I wasn't allowed to walk there with my siblings because kindergarten students were required to ride the bus. On the ill-fated morning, Mommy chased me all around the kitchen trying to dress me as my siblings laughed at my terror. "The bus isn't bad," one **quipped**, "except for the snakes." Another added, "Sometimes the bus never brings you home." Guffaws all around.

Why do the boy's siblings tell him those things about the bus?

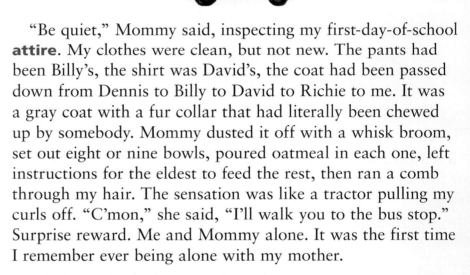

"Be quiet," Mommy said, inspecting my first-day-of-school **attire**. My clothes were clean, but not new. The pants had been Billy's, the shirt was David's, the coat had been passed down from Dennis to Billy to David to Richie to me. It was a gray coat with a fur collar that had literally been chewed up by somebody. Mommy dusted it off with a whisk broom, set out eight or nine bowls, poured oatmeal in each one, left instructions for the eldest to feed the rest, then ran a comb through my hair. The sensation was like a tractor pulling my curls off. "C'mon," she said, "I'll walk you to the bus stop." Surprise reward. Me and Mommy alone. It was the first time I remember ever being alone with my mother.

It became the high point of my day, a memory so sweet it is burned into my mind like a tattoo, Mommy walking me to the bus stop and every afternoon picking me up, standing on the corner of New Mexico and 114th Road, clad in a brown coat, her black hair tied in a colorful scarf, watching with the rest of the parents as the yellow school bus swung around the corner and came to a stop with a hiss of air brakes.

How does being picked up after school by Mommy make the narrator feel?

Gradually, as the weeks passed and the terror of going to school **subsided**, I began to notice something about my mother, that she looked nothing like the other kids' mothers.

In fact, she looked more like my kindergarten teacher, Mrs. Alexander, who was white. Peering out the window as the bus rounded the corner and the front doors flew open, I noticed that Mommy stood apart from the other mothers, rarely speaking to them. She stood behind them, waiting calmly, hands in her coat pockets, watching **intently** through the bus windows to see where I was, then smiling and waving as I yelled my greeting to her through the window. She'd quickly grasp my hand as I stepped off the bus, ignoring the stares of the black women as she whisked me away.

One afternoon as we walked home from the bus stop, I asked Mommy why she didn't look like the other mothers.

"Because I'm not them," she said.

"Who are you?" I asked.

"I'm your mother."

"Then why don't you look like Rodney's mother, or Pete's mother? How come you don't look like me?"

She sighed and shrugged. She'd obviously been down this road many times. "I do look like you. I'm your mother. You ask too many questions. Educate your mind. School is important. Forget Rodney and Pete. Forget their mothers. You remember school. Forget everything else. Who cares about Rodney and Pete! When they go one way, you go the other way. Understand? When they go one way, you go the other way. You hear me?"

"Yes."

"I know what I'm talking about. Don't follow none of them around. You stick to your brothers and sisters, that's it. Don't tell nobody your business neither!" End of discussion.

A couple of weeks later the bus dropped me off and Mommy was not there. I panicked. Somewhere in the back of my mind was the memory of her warning me, "You're going to have to learn to walk home by yourself," but that memory blinked like a distant fog light in a stormy sea and it drowned in my panic. I was lost. My house was two blocks away, but it might as well have been ten miles because I had no idea where it was.

I stood on the corner and bit back my tears. The other parents regarded me sympathetically and asked me my address, but I was afraid to tell them. In my mind was Mommy's warning, drilled into all twelve of us children from the time we could walk: "Never, ever, ever tell your business to nobody," and I shook my head no, I don't know my address. They departed one by one, until a sole figure remained, a black father, who stood in front of me with his son, saying, "Don't worry, your mother is coming soon." I ignored him. He was blocking my view, the tears clouding my vision as I tried to peer behind him, looking down the block to see if that familiar brown coat and white face would appear in the distance. It didn't.

In fact there wasn't anyone coming at all, except a bunch of kids and they certainly didn't look like Mommy. They were a motley crew of girls and boys, ragged, with wild hairdos and unkempt jackets, hooting and making noise, and only when they were almost upon me did I recognize the faces of my elder siblings and my little sister Kathy who trailed behind them. I ran into their arms and collapsed in tears as they gathered around me, laughing.

Why didn't the boy's mother pick him up?

Talking About the Story

Have students summarize what happens when the narrator gets off the bus. Then have them discuss if they think it is just by chance that the narrator's siblings show up at the bus stop on the day that Mommy does not.

Ask students to talk about the first time they remember their parents letting them do something on their own.

Words From the Story

quip

In the story, the boy's siblings quip that there are snakes on the bus and that it never brings you home. To quip means to say something that you intend to be funny and clever.

- Ask students when you might make a quip, when you are trying to make your friend smile or when you are trying to make an adult take you seriously. Explain your answer.
- Have students describe a time they answered their mother or father with a quip.

attire

In the story, the boy's mother inspects his attire on his first day of school. Your attire is the clothes you are wearing.

- Ask students which is attire, a girl's teeth or a girl's dress. Explain why.
- Have students point to one piece of their attire.

subside

After a few weeks, the boy's fear of going to school subsides. If a condition subsides, it gets less serious and begins to go away.

- Ask what is more likely to subside, mucus at the beginning of a cold or mucus at the end of a cold. Why do you think so?
- Have students demonstrate clapping that starts loud and then gradually subsides.

intent

In the story, the boy's mother watches the bus windows intently to see if she can spot her son. If you are intent on something, you concentrate very hard on it.

- Ask students where a cat might be intent, sitting by a window watching a bird outside or under a bed falling asleep. Why?
- Have students look intently at your pointing finger for twenty seconds.

Vocabulary in Action

Words About the Story

burden

In the story, the boy is very worried about going to school. You could say that his fear of school is a burden. A burden is a heavy load or something that causes you a lot of worry or work.

- Ask students which is a burden, a big suitcase filled with clothes or a small glass of water. Explain.
- Have students pretend they are carrying a burden.

foreboding

In the story, the boy is terrified that something bad will happen when he goes to school. In other words, he feels foreboding. If you feel foreboding, you feel like something very bad is going to happen.

- Ask students who feels foreboding, a girl who is excited about going on vacation or a boy who is concerned about crossing a busy street. Explain your answer.
- Have students use facial expressions and body language to express feelings of foreboding.

solace

The boy feels better when his mother says she will walk with him to the bus. Another way to say that is that his mother is a solace to him. Something that is a solace comforts you and makes you feel less sad.

- Ask students what you might take solace in, a mean comment from a bully or a warm hug from your father. Explain why.
- Have students name something that is a solace to them.

heed

In the story, the boy does not tell anyone his address because he was listening when his mother advised him not to tell anyone his business. In other words, the boy heeds the advice his mother gave him. If you heed something or someone, you pay attention to them or what they say.

- Ask students who they should heed, a firefighter or a stranger. Why?
- Have students tell about a piece of advice they heed.

Bibliography

Alexander, Lloyd. (1977). "The Cat and the Golden Egg," from *The Town Cats and Other Tales*. Illustrated by Laszlo Kubinyi. New York: Puffin Books.

Armstrong, Lance. (2000). *It's Not About the Bike: My Journey Back to Life*. New York: The Berkeley Publishing Group.

Broadwater, Andrea. (2000). *Marian Anderson: Singer and Humanitarian*. Berkeley Heights, NJ: Enslow Publishers.

Burns, Diane L. (2005). "The Mop Bucket Encore," from *Cricket*, Vol. 32, No. 5. Peru, IL: Carus Publishing Company.

Carroll, Lewis. (1871). *Through the Looking-Glass*. Mineola, NY: Dover Publications.

Clough, Sandra. (2005). "The Wisdom of Goats," from *Cricket*, Vol. 32, No. 9. Peru, IL: Carus Publishing Company.

Dahl, Roald. (1953). "The Wish," from *Skin and Other Stories*. New York: Penguin Putnam Books for Young Readers.

Freedman, Russell. (1987). *Lincoln: A Photobiography*. Boston: Houghton Mifflin Company.

Gardner, Mona. (1941). "The Dinner Party," from *Elements of Literature: First Course*. Austin, TX: Holt, Rinehart and Winston.

Griffith, Helen V. (1987). *Journal of a Teenage Genius*. New York: HarperCollins.

Gruppen, Louise. (2004). "Geoffrey Pyke's Cool Idea," from *Cricket*, Vol. 32, No. 3. Peru, IL: Carus Publishing Company.

Handwerk, Brian. (2004). "GPS Technology Drives Global Treasure Hunt," from *National Geographic News*. http://news.nationalgeographic.com/

Hernandez, David. (2000). "Happiness Epidemic," from *Free Lunch: A Poetry Miscellany*, Issue 23. Glenview, IL: Free Lunch Arts Alliance.

Lithgow, John. (2003). *I'm a Manatee*. Illustrated by Ard Hoyt. New York: Simon & Schuster Children's Publishing.

McBride, James. (1996). *The Color of Water: A Black Man's Tribute to His White Mother*. New York: Riverhead Books.

Miller, Goldman. (2003). "Beetle Blisters," from *Cricket*, Vol. 31, No. 1. Peru, IL: Carus Publishing Company.

Owen, James. (2005). "Elephants Can Mimic Traffic, Other Noises, Study Says," from *National Geographic News*. http://news.nationalgeographic.com/

Pinkney, Andrea Davis. (1998). *Duke Ellington: The Piano Prince and His Orchestra*. Illustrated by Brian Pinkney. New York: Hyperion.

Rushin, Steve. (2005). "Blindly He Goes. . . Up," from *Sports Illustrated*, Vol. 103, Issue 3. New York: Time Warner Company.

Shiflet, Carla. (2005). "Summer Plans." Austin, TX: Steck-Vaughn.

Soto, Gary. (1990). "La Bamba," from *Baseball in April and Other Stories*. Orlando, FL: Harcourt Books.

Twain, Mark. (1876). *The Adventures of Tom Sawyer*. Berkeley, CA: University of California Press.

White, E. B. (1952). *Charlotte's Web*. Illustrated by Garth Williams. New York: HarperCollins.

Additional Favorite Read-Alouds

Anaya, Rudolfo. (1999). *My Land Sings: Stories from the Rio Grande*. Illustrated by Amy Córdova. New York: HarperCollins.

Eliot, T. S. (1982). *Old Possum's Book of Practical Cats*. Illustrated by Edward Gorey. Orlando, FL: Harcourt Books.

Erickson, John R. (1983). *The Further Adventures of Hank the Cowdog*. Illustrated by Gerald L. Holmes. New York: Puffin Books.

Friedman, Amy. (1995). *The Spectacular Gift and Other Tales from Tell Me a Story*. Illustrated by Jillian H. Gilliland. Kansas City, MO: Andrews McMeel Publishing.

Griffiths, Andy. (2003). *Just Annoying!*. Illustrated by Terry Denton. New York: Scholastic.

Hoose, Phillip. (2001). *We Were There, Too!: Young People in U.S. History*. New York: Farrar, Straus and Giroux Publishers.

Lewis, C. S. (1950). *The Lion, the Witch and the Wardrobe*. Illustrated by Pauline Baynes. London: Collins Publishing Group Children's Division.

Plantz, Connie. (2001). *Bessie Coleman: First Black Woman Pilot*. Berkeley Heights, NJ: Enslow Publishers.

Prelutsky, Jack (ed). (1999). *20th Century Children's Poetry Treasury*. Illustrated by Meilo So. New York: Random House Children's Books.